A TREE BY A STREAM

Unlock the Secrets of Active Meditation

EDMOND SMITH

CHRISTIAN FOCUS PUBLICATIONS

To my wife Kerryn,
and to Neil, Howard and Ken,
who have closed ranks around me in their encouragement.

A survey was carried out among fifty elderly
citizens, who were aged ninety-five and over.
They were asked: 'What would you change if you
had another chance?' Amongst other things, they
nearly all said they would take time to think more.

© 1995 Edmond Smith
ISBN 1-85792-124-0

Published by
Christian Focus Publications Ltd
Geanies House, Fearn, Ross-shire,
IV20 1TW, Scotland, Great Britain.

Cover design by Keith Jackson
Illustration by Brady Senior

Printed and bound in Great Britain by
The Guernsey Press Co. Ltd., Vale, Guernsey, C.I.

Contents

1. WHAT IS TRUE SPIRITUAL MEDITATION? 4

2. RICHARD BAXTER 23

3. JOHN FLAVEL 38

4. JOHN BUNYAN 60

5. NATHANIEL MATHER 88

6. JOHN CALVIN 106

7. ROBERT MURRAY M'CHEYNE 126

8. JOHN NEWTON 147

9. MARTYN LLOYD-JONES 163

CONCLUSION 191

WHAT IS TRUE SPIRITUAL MEDITATION?

For some it may appear strange that in considering meditation we first look at the subject of sin and the sinner. The reaction may be: 'I am a Christian who wants to learn to meditate and you do not need to remind me I am saved from sin and that sinners – those who are outside of Christ – will perish.' That may be so, but have you thought deeply about what you mostly think on? You say you are a believer in Christ, but are you truly guided by the counsel of God or by the counsel of the world?

Do you see the counsel of the world as neutral advice or do you see it as counsel of the wicked? I once heard a preacher expound Psalm One, who in speaking about the people of the world urging a Christian to do this and do that, said, 'But, of course, the people of the world are not trying to be nasty when they urge you to do such things'. The preacher obviously reckoned the world's advice is neutral, but is it? Is it not the counsel of the wicked? Is not anything that prevents us from thinking on and doing the will of God wicked? Consider this in a world where, electronically or otherwise, we are bombarded with endless information, much of which is useless. What we may consider neutral or harmless is actually wicked if it prevents us from meditating on the law of the Lord with the kind of thinking which carries us on to do His will with delight.

The question is not so much: 'Is our time of meditation and prolonged thinking in terms of hours much the same as the hours we spend on other things?' The question is: 'Do the things of God possess our mind most of all by far?'

The things of God will possess your mind most of all only when you are aware that any counsel outside of God's counsel is wicked. All unbelievers are dangerously sinful. Certainly through the sovereign and providential rule of God they may help a believer at times despite themselves, but as sinners they are sold to sin in their mind, in their will and in their understanding. The Scripture calls unbelievers 'wicked', and therefore we should always view them as such. Never mind what they call themselves, their ways are the polar opposite to good. The unbeliever has what one Christian of old called 'disordered affections'. The natural man's desires drive him to do the things he does far more than his reason does. His conduct is governed by disordered desires. Once this is realized, meditation is seen as a vital bulwark against both the overt and the insidious ways of the world.

All this helps us to understand the opening verses of Psalm One, which has been seen by many observers as the introduction to all the Psalms. The author of Psalm One writes:

> Blessed is the man
>> who does not walk in the counsel of the wicked
> Nor stands in the way of the sinners
>> nor sits in the seat of mockers.

One can see that the godly man therefore is blessed not only because of what he does, but also because of what he does not do. He is blessed because he thinks on God's ways, but he is also blessed because he refuses wicked advice. One cannot help feeling the worth of God's law is esteemed all the more when the sinners' advice and counsel has been clearly seen as foolish. It is impossible to apply our mind to true spiritual meditation unless we are prepared to withdraw and separate from the company and influence of unbelievers. We must lock out the things of this sinful world before we can lock in the things of God. Think of where you often sit, whose company you are in – it says much about you.

We of the electronic age have much trouble with prolonged thinking. Television discourages it. The average length of any news story is 45 seconds, thus depriving the viewer of any chance of weighing up the story's implications. Public figures are known more by their looks than what they think in these times. The average length of a shot on television is only 3.5 seconds, so that the eye never rests and always has something new it must see. Christians have allowed themselves to come under the spell of electronic images and spend many hours dazzled by them. They, like the rest of the world, have come to accept the adage 'A picture is worth a thousand words'. Thus, even to read the words of the Bible may prove difficult for many Christians nowadays, let alone the effort required to contemplate in a serious way the meaning of the words. *The seemingly unsensational process of meditation is what Christians must relearn in our modern culture if they are to prove fruitful and to become content.*

Naturally, the blessing of God springs more from the delight in the meditation of the law of the Lord (for us now the whole of His Word in both the Old and the New Testaments) than in rejecting the counsel and the company of unbelievers. So the author of Psalm One states:

> But (the godly man's) delight is in the law of the LORD,
> and on his law he meditates day and night.

Because God's Word is viewed as law, it certainly makes meditation imperative, and it is not to be divorced from vigorous application to one's own life and circumstances. The law consists of precepts, instructions and teaching (see *Amplified Bible* on Psalm 1:2). *Precepts* are rules of action and behaviour. *Instructions* as a word applies to orders that may not be contravened and often carries the meaning of doing that which has been learnt by heart and which one intends to perform more than once. When one looks at the Bible, one certainly is impressed with its detailed instruction. (It takes about 50 hours to read the Old Testament and 20 hours to read the New.) *Teachings* refers to the multiple-guided process outlined in the Word. Whilst some of God's children may be exasperated when God's guidance is sought – thinking the Bible does not give adequate light at all times – maturity leads us to learn that the Word is sufficient in detail insofar as it gives us all the principles of life we need, and so sheds much light on the practical too.

Since God's Word carries instructions, details, precepts of a systematic nature, meditation therefore requires an acquaintance with all the aspects of salvation that such a system suggests. To meditate with this in mind, a believer needs to trace God's dealings with mankind through the Fall, through the Flood, through the choice of Israel as the nation to bring in universal blessing, the preparation for the Messiah through the Old Testament sacrificial system, the Davidic kingdom, the disobedience and failure of Israel, the promise of a new covenant, and so on, until one traces the times leading up to the First Advent of Christ, with all that followed on from that. All this, however, must be applied to the reader's own times. Too often the Word is not applied in this way and believers wonder why the Word loses its thrill.

Meditation, applying the Word through prolonged and vigorous application, can be likened to a lock. We lock out godless counsel, we lock in the things of God, and meditation is the lock itself. Many moderns in Western countries have become alarmed at the high and rising incidence of burglaries of private homes over the last decade; but would we as believers take as much care to lock out the evil of this age in our mind! Meditation is a time lock as well. When the evil of this world bombards the minds of Christians and the evil seems like getting through, then the time given to meditation on the things of God is one more impediment that threatening ungodliness must overcome. It is a lock using time to keep out the unwanted, as well as guarding the treasured law of the Lord in the mind.

The writer of the first psalm has us thinking about meditation in the light of men's destinies. Christianity is presented as a heap of fun too often in our times, but eternal destinies hang on what people think about and what that thinking leads them to do and become in this life:

> (The godly man) is like a tree planted by streams of water,
> > which yields its fruit in season
> and whose leaf does not wither.
> > Whatever he does prospers.
> Not so the wicked!
> > They are like chaff
> > that the wind blows away.
> Therefore the wicked shall not stand in the judgement,
> > nor sinners in the assembly of the righteous.
> For the LORD watches over the way of the righteous,
> > but the way of the wicked shall perish.

One can see that meditation is thinking ahead. It is making plans and taking definite action. The man who meditates day and night constantly draws from God's Word and becomes like a tree by a stream. Water secretly causes the tree to thrive – yet the work of the water is not observable. Meditation is a secret, hidden occupation – it does not go on parade – but the blessing of it becomes apparent and bears fruit. Its fruit is not secret even if its source is. *Meditation will lead to a calmness of disposition, a serenity of mind, and a certainty about the ways of God.* Whatever happens to the believer who meditates is perceived by the Psalmist as being conducive to his salvation somehow, until he stands in the assembly of the righteous in the glory to come.

In the past God indeed has given His people men who could discern the difference between what is of God and what is wicked. These men were true champions of the Faith, some of them standing alone in their generation. They proved fruitful in themselves and fruitful in their labours for others. Interestingly enough, they are men whose names have been deeply etched in the memories of their ensuing generations, among believers and unbelievers alike. In the following pages we shall look at some of these outstanding men, proving that meditation is that which leads to enviable blessing.

Wending our way through the Word

Although it pays to read the choice works of or about great Christians to realize the potential there is for meditation, we must not be overawed by such great figures. While God gives some men extraordinary ability to dig and delve into His Word, we ought to see that although ours may not be the gift to excavate as deeply, we all can dig to levels of satisfaction to ourselves.

To change the metaphor, we are all called by God to wend our own way through His Word. I suggest there is a definite, most effective way of doing this in order to cover all the territory we should. To put it simply: we should read all of God's Word and become familiar with it all, and we should also meditate on all of it.

How shall we achieve this as successfully as possible? To take one step at a time, let us consider the subject of reading all of God's Word.

All of God's Word needs to be read regularly over a relatively short period of time. Lloyd-Jones was accustomed to reading the

Bible through in one year. He thought that as Christians it is the least we can do. If that is true, then many believers do not perform the least. Many of us may appease ourselves with the thought that we read many Christian and spiritual books, but nothing can truly take the place of being familiar with the God-breathed Word. *It is too easy to read books about the Word and not read the Word itself.* We are blessed, I believe, if we arrive at this conclusion: 'There's so much of the Scripture to read that there is hardly any time to read a Christian book'. Bible calendars and even One Year Bibles are purchasable to make it easy to read the Scriptures through in the relatively short time of a year.

We cannot meditate as we ought if we do not have sufficient knowledge on which to base our thoughts. Spiritual meditation of the right kind may include reflecting gratefully on God's providential ways with us, may include the interpretation of our present circumstances, may include with great pleasure reminiscing on the way the Lord initially saved us. But any meditation of the right kind is that which is based on God's Word and seeks to conform and interpret according to it. The Word needs to be the stabilizing influence on what we think.

Since I will suggest that meditation of the most fruitful kind is that which is performed without a Bible being open before you, it will be readily seen that a knowledge of the supremely-inspired Scriptures ought to be a growingly thorough one. Only the constant reading of all of the Word can ensure this will be so.

With respect to having a comprehensive knowledge of all Scriptures, I came to the realization around 1989 that my existing method at that time of studiously reading rather minute parts of books of the Bible meant it was going to take me years to get through a good part of the Scriptures — a few verses, or a paragraph each day with sixty-six books to cover was not going to get me far. That is why I bought a One Year Bible and sought to make the reading of it a minimum for study of the Scriptures.

Now the second step. We should not only wend our way through all of God's Word by reading it all over a relatively short time, but as we wend our way through it all we ought to meditate on it all as well. '*All* Scripture is God-breathed...' and therefore ought to be comprehensively reflected on.

Baxter's method of meditating on the subject of heaven may be an excellent starting point for the aspiring meditator when knowledge of the Scriptures is not all that broad. It does not matter what book, what chapter and verse of the Bible is the origin of your thoughts, go ahead and think about all you know on what the Bible teaches about heaven. Attempt it without having the Bible open before you. Sounds difficult? Try it, and spend ten minutes engaged in such thinking. Do not be put off by distractions – they are bound to come, especially if your mind is not accustomed to sustained thinking. Push on undeterred. You will be surprised after ten minutes at what you know, and surprised at the lasting impression the Word of God has made on you. Then attempt on other occasions other broad subjects, such as The Nature of God, Creation, The New Birth, The Crucifixion, Election to Salvation and The Second Coming. How vivid will such subjects be to you!

Memorization of Scripture is a powerful kind of meditation. Anyone who has taken to learning verses and even chapters of the Bible knows that every word – be it noun, verb, adjective or whatever – leaps out at you as you memorize, and you feel them all as you seek to be word perfect in your recall.

I suggest, however, there is a better and happier way of meditating than to reflect on broad subjects or to memorize isolated verses and chapters of Scripture. *The finest meditation takes place without the Bible being open before you as a reflection on the things of God according to the overall way they have been written in His Word.* We do well to reflect on Creation and such like, and to memorize some of the Word without paying much heed to its context, but we ought to think in terms of the various books of the Bible with respect to the contents of each, the substance of the chapters, and the sequence of thought as well as the logic of thought.

Are we able, for instance, to go through the whole of Ephesians in our mind without referring to the letter? Do we know how the letter begins? Do we know the spiritual blessings Paul writes about, the blessings connected with the work of the Father and the Son and the Holy Spirit? Then, what follows after Paul mentions such blessings? Yes, there is thanksgiving and prayer. What is the substance of Paul's prayer for the Ephesian Christians? There are three things he prays they may know when they are further enlightened – what are they? Then what follows Paul's prayer? Yes, there is the reminder of what they were once. What is the substance of his writing on this point? On and on we go until we reach the end of Paul's great letter.

This type of meditation may appear daunting for many, but such an approach is paying heed to the design of God's Word. Many believers have perhaps used this approach on a smaller scale as they have read systemically small sequential passages from the Scriptures each day. Yet a most contented approach is to meditate without an open Bible on the whole contents of biblical books according to the sequence of thought. If one is fairly unfamiliar with the Word, such an approach will not meet with success overnight. Naturally, a seasoned believer, who has been reading the Scriptures for years, will profit most from this practice. All the same, the most ignorant of believers ought to take heart and be assured they know more than they realise.

As far as can be ascertained, this method of meditation has not been advocated by any great thinking Christians, such as the men surveyed in this book. Nevertheless it is putting into practice the kind of approach used towards the Scriptures by the likes of Dr Lloyd-Jones, for one, in preaching.

It is a most satisfying discipline because it means that one can go throughout the Word of God far more than once a year. Even reading the Word through annually in itself may mean seeing many parts of it only once a year, and thinking just a little on much of it for a brief moment once a year. *Meditating on the contents of whole books of the Bible can ensure a considerable familiarity with much of it quite a number of times in a year, particularly if one sets out to study and recall one different book a day.*

We ought to be able to contemplate on the contents of the Word without having it open. It needs to be reiterated: many of us would be surprised at what we already know if we took the time to do it. Some may rejoin: 'Why bother to recall it when the knowledge is already there?' Two answers come to mind: (a) in recalling what we know we are assured we definitely possess such knowledge; (b) in seeking to recall we also discover what we do not know, perhaps discover we do not know what we thought we knew. Such knowledge needs to surface in order to be appreciated and addressed.

In countries accustomed to so many Bibles being available to everyone, it may be difficult to understand the importance of meditating without the open Bible. Yet suppose we are living in a land where suddenly Bibles have vanished because the authorities have both forbidden and confiscated them. How will we fare? In such a land, suppose we come across two believers who have known the Lord for the same number of years, and one of them, despite not now possessing a Bible, obviously knows it well and can either recite or tell you much about its actual words, while the other believer can recall very little. Need we ask who of the two will capture your admiration? Will you not rightly conclude that the knowledgeable Christian had not only read the Word, but had thought much about it as well? Will you not rightly conclude that the ignorant believer had not seriously taken God's Word to heart, that it likely had not moved him in his inmost being to desire greatly the things divine?

The confiscation of the Scriptures is not a hypothetical circumstance in some countries, and it is lovely to read of believers in such places who take the Word to heart. In Ralph Toliver's enthralling book *Gold Fears No Fire*, the author tells the story of two young Chinese men herded to work by soldiers with fixed bayonets. One, Noble Heart, has discovered another believer in the dehumanizing camp. He catches up with him as they trudge to the rubber plantation. Noble Heart says, 'Repeat John three again today. You left out part of it yesterday.' So Helang began: 'There was a man of the Pharisees, named Nicodemus ...'. The next day 'it would be Helang's turn to drill Noble Heart'. If they disagreed over the memory work, they would hide behind a rubber tree and consult the text itself.

Persecution, hardship, does wonderful things to believers, but whether or not we face it, the Word must live in us, not fly by us. It must not be merely tasted or sampled, but digested to know the pleasure of its goodness.

Memorization of various parts of Scripture is a great aid to meditating on the contents of biblical books. Although memorization centres on isolated verses and chapters, memorization can take the guiding parental hand of meditation and travel farther into the regions of the Word. To express it another way, it can become a pivotal point around which the believer can hang the tapestry of that particular part of God's revelation. Many believers know Ephesians 2:8–9 by heart. It becomes more wonderful to the mind if the believer is able to recall – not word for word necessarily, but some phrases, some expressions and the drift of the Apostle's argument – the whole of Ephesians 2:1–11 at least. If he knows what precedes 2:1–11, even better. If he knows what follows 2:1–11, then he is mastering the Word well according to the way the Spirit guided Paul's pen long ago. Ephesians 2:8–9 is not a key verse *per se* but it can be a key which opens the door for our memory to what Paul says by way of context.

As well as memorizing Scripture as an aid for comprehensive meditation on all the Word, outlines of the various books can help too as pins on which to hang the tapestry. Gifted biblical expositors have provided useful outlines in commentaries. An example of a useful outline of 1 John is : The Seven Contrasts.

1. Light v. darkness (1:5–2:11)
2. Father v. the world (2:12–2:17)
3. Christ v. the antichrist (2:18–2:28)
4. Good works v. evil works (2:29–3:24)
5. Holy Spirit v. error (4:1–4:16)
6. Love v. pious pretence (4:17–4:21)
7. God-born v. others (5:1–5:21)

Although some outlines may appear stilted to the purists, and although such outlines are not strictly divinely inspired, they are very useful if they are memorized and they never outlive their purpose. The more knowledgeable one becomes in the Word of God, the more useful such outlines and divisions can be. As one progresses in the truth, there is more knowledge to put under each heading.

Of course, meditation is not merely an intellectual pursuit, a quest to attain encyclopaedic knowledge. As George Swinnock, a Puritan, wrote: 'Our design in meditation must be rather to cleanse our hearts than to clear our heads'. *Meditation in all circumstances ought to be geared towards stirring up our feelings for the things of God, to the point where we delight in them, and seek the Father in prayer as we apply the truth to our hearts.*

Prayer grows out of sound meditation. George Swinnock likened believers to certain large birds which need a good run-up before they take to the air – meditation gives us the good run-up before we take flight and engage in prayer with God.

Consider Ephesians 2 once more. We can ask ourselves all kinds of questions as we strive to recall all we know of the chapter. It may be easy to recall the content of the chapter without any degree of difficulty and forget to apply the truth.

* Do I remember following the ways of the world and can I recall how dead I was? (Think in what ways you yourself revealed how dead you were.)
* Do I remember I was disobedient and do I now look on anybody who is an unbeliever without sentimentality and see them as disobedient?
* Do I truly agree all who are outside of Christ are objects of His wrath?
* Do I really feel God's love is great?
* Do I see other believers equally as objects of His mercy?
* Is it not possible that the unbelievers I know could become objects of His rich mercy as well?

How could one not pray as he asked such questions as these! As we realize anew how fading are our impressions of the awful destiny of sinners, of the astounding love of God, and so on, we shall always be begging God to renew us, to put before our mind similar sentiments to those experienced by the writer of Psalm 1, who takes us to the true end of meditation when he reminds us of the certain prosperity of the godly, the futile end of sinners, and that God knows the way of the righteous but the way of the wicked will perish.

It is glorious to think constantly on the things of God, to have such things possess you and mould you for His glory. It is wonderful to have the objective truths of God's Word take hold of us and cause us to know 'the science' of what happened to make salvation in Christ possible in the whole course of history, to know 'the science' of what happens when we turn to Christ in faith for deliverance from sin and damnation, to know 'the science' of what will happen at His Second Coming to make such a salvation complete.

Thanks for the memory
As you acquaint yourself through much thought on all of the God-breathed writings, you will gain countless precious impressions, insights both into the Word itself and the providential ways of the Lord in your life. It seems a logical step to consider keeping a spiritual diary.

Just as the Scriptures are in many ways a kind of diary of the adventures of God's people in the past, so your diary becomes an account of your adventures on the way to heaven. Our own diaries will be fallible works – the record of a rash judgment proved later to be wrong, exaggerated feelings, and so on – but they can reflect how faithfully God is dealing with us, how we are progressing in the Faith, the heartaches and the joys we have known, the promises the Father has given us, the answered prayers and the like. All our experiences will blessedly blend with much that we find in the Word, only it is our own account of how God has dealt individually with us.

So, as we wend our way to heaven there are three profitable things we can do: read the Word well, think on it much, and write frequently about its impressions on us.

I have kept a spiritual diary since 1986, and my deep regret is that I did not begin one much further back. I have found John

Flavel's appeal for diary-writing a sound one, to see at firsthand how the mystery of providence has touched my life.

When you keep a diary, you will discover it is a sober means of assessing yourself. Diary-keeping will not make you immune to pride and conceit, but you will be subject to far less pride and conceit when you take note of your actions and reactions to the events of each day. This matter ought not to be underestimated. We live in days when talk about pride, self-esteem and self-confidence is rife and there is not enough talk about humility, self-worth in terms of modesty, and self-examination. Many Christians are frightened of putting themselves down and thinking too much about sin, but the true believer, while he ought to have a healthy image of himself, knows that the only healthy image is the one to be had in Christ – we are to be concerned more with His glory than our own self-preservation. Therefore, the true believer can afford to open up to the Holy Spirit, who for the sake of our holiness not only encourages us, but exposes our sins and shows us the emptiness of some of our pursuits and throws light on our motives.

Of interest in diary-keeping is our observation of other people as well as ourselves. To the casual observer many things other people do to them or around them pass by without very much analysis. It is not for us to prejudge others and draw false presumptions, but there are many occasions when men are known by their fruits, as our Saviour observed. Our diaries are private works, but if we are referring to other people, then we could well copy the ways of our forefathers in the Faith and use blanks for others' names, or merely use the first letter of their name followed by a blank.

Why tread softly without exposing others' names if the diary is private? Well, one of the blessings of a good diary is the eventual benefit it will be for other people – this is a point Flavel makes. Flavel is careful to note we should not write down everything – 'religion does not lay all open' – but what we write can later on be of benefit to the church of God.

We need to remember too that if meditation is such a blessing to the believer, it stands to reason Satan will launch fierce attacks on the mind, and we need to cope adequately with such attacks. If we seek to think on the things of God, he will seek to prevent us from doing so. John Bunyan wrestled with this difficulty when he touched on the subject of meditation.

Satan would force us into meditation of another kind. Still, such meditation can be turned on its head and used to our advantage when we stand our ground and answer him according to the truth of God's grace. We may think it is silly that a believer, mature and well-experienced in the joys of believing in the gospel, could become a despondent man all of a sudden, that such a man would be forced to go right back to the fundamentals of the gospel. But Bunyan is correct. Such a man is forced to look again, both at the truth and the fact of the existence of sin, original sin, the evil of sin, the ongoing need of salvation. It is as if the grown man becomes a baby again.

Satan will often be attacking, but sometimes he is particularly crafty and subtle in his evil intent. There is the fierce and full attack he makes at times, when the attack comes unexpectedly, it comes contrary to our greatest wishes and strongest hopes. It is then that the subject of our usual meditation may have to be displaced by what appear as the more babyish matters: does sin really exist in the world or is it a figment of the imagination? Is sin really as bad as the Word depicts it? Are all religions ways to God? Is Christ truly unique? Normally, the meditating believer knows the answers well and with a great degree of certainty, but when Satan overtly and suddenly attacks him, doubt breeds hideous uncertainty. One feels quite helpless in such a circumstance, knowing that until God comes in His mercy, one is at the mercy of Satan no matter how many onslaughts he has faced before.

It is best to not only meet Satan face-to-face with both Scripture and our own experience of salvation, but to set out in the diary all the answers that can be employed to meet Satan's objections, accusations and assumptions. Satan is a good apologist for his own cause, but he can be met by a Christian apology, which can stand up to his test.

I well remember experiencing a sudden attack by Satan through an article I read in a national newspaper, an article which questioned the historicity of Jesus. Despair rolled over me, but I decided through meditation to set my thoughts out according to real and spiritual logic. In writing out my answers to that assault I quickly dispensed with the doubt and re-established my assurance. I have much pleasure in occasionally going back to that part of my diary and re-reading that which helped to disperse the doubt. Memory does not keep all that is given to me, but many things have been written and become precious memories able to be recalled when needed.

In some sense I see the keeping of a spiritual diary to be on a similar plane as the preservation of God's written word as found in the Old and New Testaments. God has not only honoured the spoken word but the written word as well. In fact, the spoken word has been enshrined in the written to preserve it. God could not trust men's minds to preserve by oral tradition what He had revealed. The revelation had to be recorded with pen and ink and paper lest it be forgotten by noble minds or corrupted by twisted minds. God's Word underlines the truth that much that is objectively good and dear can be lost if it is not written down.

Anyone who has read Bunyan's *Grace Abounding to the Chief of Sinners* can see that Satan went to a seventeenth-century man with really the same questions he uses to plant doubt in the mind of any man of any century. Thus the book will always prove to be an inestimable blessing to believers of any age, and in particular to those who face any of Satan's overt attacks. In many ways it was Bunyan's diary.

Satan somehow sensed what damage Bunyan would do to his cause if he overcame doubt and became a sure and solid believer, so he attacked him sorely, just as he seeks to bring destruction to any serious meditator. When the soil is fertile, it can be the means of profusive and great growth of wanted and unwanted plants. On the natural plane, the man who can imagine the best and be among the best at doing it, is the same man who can imagine the worst and be among the best at doing that as well. In short, our strength can become our weakness. He who meditates is he who is adept at imagining the best, but Satan is quick to take advantage of such a man and cast him down to the lowest depths when he had been on the heights. As far as I know, Bunyan did not suggest the believer keep a diary, but many of his fellow-Puritans did, and he himself must have derived much benefit for himself by writing out 'Grace Abounding', as well as making it a blessing to so many others.

A diary ought to be written with a certain degree of expectancy. If God gives us a promise from His Word, impresses us with His power to perform a certain thing, then we should note down the promise and then watch to see how He will bring about the fulfilment. *It is marvellous how the Lord times events to make His Word come true, and it is good for us to write about it, as there will be times to come when despair will threaten us and we need to recall His past mercies.* Is it unreasonable to think that the more we think on His Word, the more promises we will be given? Is it unreasonable to think that the more we thankfully take note of how He fulfilled any promises given to us, the more promises He will add to those already given?

It stands to reason that Satan is out to get those whose meditation will produce an influence that is beyond the usual, in particular he targets preachers and teachers of the gospel. Dr Lloyd-Jones is a case in point. In 1949 he felt unable to preach. Darkness had descended on him, following closely a time when he felt exceptionally near to God. Then the words 'God who cannot lie' arrested him and overwhelmed him so that he was in tears. When the great man entered the pulpit that Sunday morning in 1949, it is noteworthy that he felt it was necessary to start his sermon with 'something great and fundamental'. The attack had taken him back to the 'something great and fundamental'.

Most of us will never reach the stature of any of the eight men who feature in this book or have the influence they had, but all who aspire to be godly are to take note of what characterized the eight of them and follow their example, as well as that found in the Scripture, particularly in Psalm 1. We all shall then be like a tree by a stream.

If we keep a diary, then much of our meditation can take a permanent form and may prove to be of benefit for others, even though we ought not to keep one with that in mind. *The Diary of Kenneth Macrae* is an excellent case in point. Kenneth Macrae was a minister of the gospel in the Free Church of Scotland congregations at Lochgilphead, Kilmuir and Stornoway early this century. Iain Murray edited Macrae's diaries and had much of the material published in a reasonably large but fascinating book. The material came from diary entries made by Macrae between 1912 and 1963! Iain Murray says: 'Only after (Macrae's) death did anyone become aware of its value to the church at large'. Macrae had not intended it for publication for he knew, as any good diarist should, diaries are first and foremost private accounts geared for our own self-examination and edification. Yet, they may be of use to others at a later time.

2

RICHARD BAXTER

Richard Baxter (1615–1691) was a Puritan. The Puritans initially formed a movement within the English Church during the reign of Elizabeth I, in the hope of making the Reformation more complete. They regarded the English Church, though somewhat reformed, as still tainted by practices of the Roman Catholic Church. They went from questioning the use of vestments, the sign of the cross, etc., to questioning eventually the right of the State to meddle in the affairs of the Church. Many of them sought an alternative church government in order to bring home to people what they believed the New Testament – as apart from tradition – actually taught. The Puritans held preaching in very high esteem, with a strong emphasis on the need for repentance and regeneration for salvation. Baxter was a Puritan giant, though some of his theology did not square up with what many other Puritans believed.

He is best known for his ministry at Kidderminster, where he pastored the people for sixteen years. There at Kidderminster he preached effectively, yet he found far more success in teaching his congregation through pastoral counselling and systematic catechizing, that is, by teaching people the basics of the Christian faith by question and answer method as he went from home to home.

He enjoyed great success at Kidderminster. One may say it was a revival. Before coming to the town he found the place was rife with ignorance and foul language. He only found a single instance or two of people practising daily prayer in any one street he visited, whereas at the close of his ministry only a single instance or two of people not practising daily prayer could be found. The number of communicants rose to 600 in the town where there were about 800 homes and 2,000 people.

> 'And on Lord's Days, instead of the open profanation to which they had been so long accustomed, a person in passing through the town in the intervals of public worship, might overhear hundreds of families engaged in singing psalms, reading the Scriptures and other good books, or such sermons as they had taken down while they heard them from the pulpit.'

Although Baxter had more confidence in his catechizing and individual instruction than in preaching, he still preached powerfully and it is to him we owe the well-known words: 'I preached as never like to preach again, and as a dying man to dying men.' He also said of preaching: 'Let the awful and important thoughts of souls being saved by my preaching, or left to perish and be condemned to hell by negligency, I say let this awful and important tremendous thought dwell ever upon your spirit.' The church was usually full at the height of his ministry and this meant there were 1,000 people attending his preaching. During his ministry at Kidderminster five galleries had to be built to accommodate his hearers.

His best-known written work is *The Reformed Pastor*. Baxter was a member of a clerical fraternity that had resolved to adopt the policy of systematic catechizing, based on his plan. On the day Baxter was to preach to the fraternity with this plan in view, he fell ill; so he published the material he had prepared, an exposition and application of Paul's words of farewell to the Ephesian elders about guarding themselves and the flock of God. He called the work *Gilda Salvianus* after two writers of the fifth and sixth centuries, who had been blunt in castigating their generation for their sins. 'By their names,' said Baxter, 'I offer you an excuse ... for plain dealing.' *The Reformed Pastor* was merely the subtitle of the work, and by 'reformed' Baxter had in mind, in good Puritan style, the need of the pastor to be renewed to serve God without any reserve. J. I. Packer, well-known contemporary evangelical writer of our time, describes the work: '*The Reformed Pastor* was, and is, dynamite, and it made its mark at once.' The book stirred many of Baxter's contemporaries to employ the same methods of catechizing their people for the sake of the gospel, and its influence was felt beyond his generation. We read of Charles Wesley and William Grimshaw, a century or more later, believing that preachers should 'visit from house to house after Mr Baxter's manner'. Baxter, with the help of two assistants, would spend every Monday and Tuesday, from morning until nightfall, taking some fifteen or sixteen families each week in the work of catechism. In one year they would visit all the families of the congregation, about 800 in all.

Even if one has decided he cannot duplicate Baxter's method of educating his congregation, *The Reformed Pastor* is still essential reading, just for its sense of urgency alone. The germ of the book lies in the solemn conviction that men without Jesus Christ are lost in sin and bound for an eternal hell unless they believe. The pastor carries an awful responsibility to urge all men to turn from their sins and be saved. The pastor cannot rest while he knows that unbelievers are going to hell. Because of this, any degree of discomfort, poverty and overwork ought to be endured.

Listen to Baxter plead on this matter: 'Is this all thy compassion for sinners? Wilt thou do no more to seek and to save them? ... Shall they die and be in hell before thou wilt speak to them one serious word to prevent it? Shall they curse thee forever that thou didst no more in time to save them?'

Baxter was very frank in *Gilda Salvianus*, true to his word. He urged that ministers should preach of eternal issues as men who truly believe and feel what they say. He insisted that church discipline be practised as well, to show that the Church is serious about sin within the Church as well as outside the Church among unbelievers.

Now, the question that ought to come to our mind is: Why was Richard Baxter so conscious and alive to eternal issues? It is true that any believing person, preacher or otherwise, ought to read *The Reformed Pastor*, and it is true that any reader of that work will be stirred into being fervent in hating sin and dreading lest he fails to tell others about Jesus and they die and go to hell. *The Reformed Pastor*, however, will not make the lasting impression it ought to make unless the reader goes to the springs of Baxter's mind and sees why and how this Puritan maintained his extraordinary sense of urgency. What convinced Baxter that heaven and hell are real? Why did heaven and hell appear real to him? Why were they so real that he became intoxicated with love for the people of the town of Kidderminster and beyond?

The answer lies in another of Baxter's works, called *The Saints' Everlasting Rest*. *The Reformed Pastor* is his best known work, but this ought not to be seen as his most important. Among Baxter's works *The Saints' Everlasting Rest* is truly the engine room. In it we see how Baxter raised himself up to think deeply, seriously, leisurely, over extended periods of time, on heaven and hell. Certainly, *The Saints' Everlasting Rest* concerns itself far more with heaven than hell – it is a work chiefly aimed to set believers thinking about the blessed hope of heaven. Yet in it there are references to hell, and it compels us to believe that Baxter's awareness of both heaven and hell arose from his ability to meditate long and hard on these eternal issues. *The Reformed Pastor* draws more attention because it concerns action. But, as the psalmist reveals in Psalm 1, proper meditation gives birth to stability and action, and the great Puritan was most conscious of this, as we shall see.

Today in certain Christian circles, even where one expects better things, conferences and meetings are held without any attention given to the importance of thinking and meditation. One such conference for Reformed preachers referred to ministerial training, the pastor as counsellor, the pastor as a man of authority, pastors and proper church government, pastors and the call to the ministry, the pastor as a biblical preacher, but not a word about the pastor as a thinker, as a meditator. To refer to one conference may seem to be the building up of brittle, selective evidence, but there are countless conferences arranged all over the world where no attention is given to this matter. Is it not 'action-packed' enough to be considered? *Yet have we never seriously considered the enormous ramifications that take place when a man becomes the kind of meditator Baxter was?*

It is not being argued that every preacher or otherwise who meditates as Baxter did will become as mighty as the great Puritan, but simply that the genuine meditator will experience in power the realities of salvation, and then could well be 'an instrument for noble purposes, made holy, useful to the Master and prepared to do any good work' (2 Tim. 2:21). *The Saints' Everlasting Rest* is not simply one of the most valuable parts of Baxter's works; as one compiler suggests – it is the most vital of all. Happily the compiler saw it as a practical work, but he should have gone on to describe it as the most practical of them all. It is interesting that the compiler in mind lived in an age when meditation was considered practical – how many believers today would call it practical? Yet, it is the light that burns the wood that makes the blazing fire.

The Saints' Everlasting Rest was published in 1650. In

between the years 1641 and 1660 Baxter was the pastor of Kidderminster, but at the time of writing *The Saints' Rest,* it is said that he was far from home and in a state of ill-health. He had served in the Cromwellian Army for a time and had returned to a place called Rouse Lench, where he wrote his unexcelled masterpiece on meditation. Apparently, for many months he expected to die. He only had his Bible with him, but as he fixed his thoughts on heaven, his thoughts were of more benefit to him 'than all the studies of my life'. He was thirty, and it was to be six years before he would write *The Reformed Pastor.* The meditations on heaven so moved him that he felt compelled to write a book on the subject, as well as giving a lecture every week to his people on the subject once he returned to Kidderminster.

Dr Bates wrote that Baxter's work as a book on meditation unveils heaven for us, as well as removing the screen to make visible the everlasting fire of hell. Some may be afraid that Baxter overreached in his imagination, but a careful study of *The Saints' Rest* reveals no such thing. While Baxter urges his readers to call on their imagination and walk around the walls of the new Jerusalem, for instance, he is merely inviting them to call up images that the Scriptures use. There is nothing wrong with being imaginative so long as our thoughts are guided by what the Word reveals. We all know imagination can be to our ruin, but we all know that in 'thinking God's thoughts after Him' our imagination can be of great blessing.

Although Roman Catholic mystics, for example, have gone to an extreme in imagining the wounds of Christ and have allegedly received stigmata or bodily wounds in themselves through thinking intently on Christ's passion, we cannot cancel out the possibility of a right use of our imaginative powers.

No-one would argue that the Creator did not give us such powers. Baxter used them as a proof that they are an excellent means of growing into true and profitable servants of Christ. If we hold that the blessed man meditates and consequently prospers, then we are compelled to think and imagine within the rule of the Word of God. In this sense Baxter says: 'The memory will not be idle, or useless, in the blessed work. From that height the saint can look before him and behind him. And to compare past with present things must raise in the blessed soul an inconceivable esteem and sense of its condition.'

Endorsements for the importance of this book have some surprising features. While written with Christians mainly in mind, it was the instrument of some conversions. For a certain minister, it inspired him to write to a relative words to the effect, 'Meditation on eternal things I count as a means to drive away mental depression. If we as Christians spent one hour a day in this serious and deep kind of meditation, and in such contemplation walked with God, it would have immeasurable influence on our whole lives. I cannot overvalue Baxter's book.'

A contemporary Puritan of Baxter's time said of him, in thinking of *The Saints' Everlasting Rest* and Baxter's own life: 'Mr Baxter is almost in heaven'. Then, there is that marvellous endorsement expressed by an eleven-year-old boy before he died: 'I pray, let me have Mr Baxter's book, that I may read a little more of eternity before I go in to it.' *The Saints' Rest* was for the eleven-year-old the most important book after the Bible! (Not only does it say much about the boy's ability to read, it speaks volumes for his spirituality.) It appears that for many who had access to *The Saints' Rest*, it became all the means of making the issues of eternity gloriously more momentous.

Now for a look at the book itself. Firstly, it is to be noted that Baxter admits to a struggle with meditation. This cannot be put down to the lack of the right temperament, lack of the right mood at the required time, or anything of that sort. No, he sees his struggle with it as one that will be common to all who will venture out in deliberate contemplation, as the struggle of that of a godly man beset with afflictions and temptations strong enough to draw him away from concentrating on the things of God. *Even if we know what blessing is in store for us once we engage in meditation, even if we have already experienced much blessing through it, the struggle is ever there.* Baxter exclaims, 'O vile nature, that resists so much, and so long, such a blessing!' Some people appear to be more reflective than others, but the Puritan would not have thought there is no struggle for such a naturally reflective person, as the one that appears to be more reflective can be distracted also and taken away from meditating on what he set out to think about. All who seek to meditate seriously are all burdened with the 'vile nature', so that Baxter could write 'Ourselves are the greatest snares to ourselves'.

Still, he bids us not to be morbid with thoughts about our vile nature, but to be convinced sufficiently of our blessed Redeemer: 'No thanks to thee, unworthy self, for this received crown.' As the believer thinks of the love of God in Christ, he finds his heart yearns, 'O that I could love Christ more!' This causes the believer to rise up and not just think of it as merely the love of God, but the *everlasting* love of God. As we are under grace, 'the passage of paradise is not now blocked up as when the law and curse reigned'. Consequently go ahead and think, believer, think on the glorious appearing of Christ, the general resurrection, the last judgment and the saints' coronation. 'Study frequently, study thoroughly this word – eternity.' Never mind if you do not know exactly how or when Christ saved you, if you are sure He has definitely done a good work, go on to contemplate all that God has in store for you by way of everlasting rest.

Only a hard heart makes heaven and hell things of little consequence. The world may accuse you of doing too much when you solemnly use the powers of your soul to think of eternity, but you know in your conscience that you are accused of doing not enough. 'God is in earnest with you, and why should you not be so with Him? Jesus Christ was serious in purchasing our redemption. (The Holy Spirit's) motions are frequent, pressing and importunate.' It is strange how some are content to be uncertain about their salvation, but if you are dangerously sick, don't you eagerly enquire of the doctor as to whether or not you will pull through and want to know if the illness will not prove to be fatal? You see, on earth the church is a hospital; we who believe are all sick and made uncertain about our assurance of salvation through indwelling sin, therefore we ought to seek the medicine that procures assurance.

Never mind what other Christians do. You could go through a congregation of a thousand men and you would find that only a few of them had ever bothered to give even one hour in a close examination of their 'title to heaven'. Never mind others, ask yourself if you have ever 'solemnly taken your heart to task'. When was the time you did it? Where was the place? Did you do it in the sight of God? Did you pass before the Scriptures as you did it? Did you take care to see if your heart is truly a new heart, if your heart is holy? Still, do not overdo the examination of the heart and become introspective and so fall for despair. 'It is far better to accept Christ as offered, than spend so much time in doubting whether we have Christ or not.'

O the fine balance we need! We ought not to look at ourselves too much and not sufficiently on Christ, and yet we must not be deluded into thinking Christ thinks little of sin. Although He ate and drank with sinners, remember He ate and drank with them as their doctor and not as their friend, says Baxter.

We need healing, and we need help to find our way home through our thoughts. Heaven is home and we should be often thinking of getting there without being distracted, otherwise we are like little children who have wandered away in our play and we have become enchanted along the way with things that stop us from finding our way back home. Let Baxter's quaint but telling words explain: 'We are like little children strayed from home, and God is now bringing us home, and we are ready to turn into any house, stay and play with everything on the way, and sit down on every green bank, and much ado there is to get us home.' If you think you are earnest about getting to heaven, stop and ask yourself if you are just as impatient of living here on earth as you are afraid of dying. Ask yourself if you are so impatient that every day seems like a year to you until the day you die – you cannot wait to die!

Are you afraid to die? Ask yourself the reason for it. We may have 'so much faith and Christianity in our mouths', but we could be all talk – deep down in our hearts there is much unfaithfulness and paganism that we hate to think about dying. If we are unwilling to die, it says much about our love for sin – if we really hate sin, we will welcome death. It is evident that we humans often put off the subject of our death! We have a whole lifetime to think about it and prepare for it, and yet we do not. We have years to spend in preparation for our death, which will come to us in one hour! We are a strange people, wanting to do the opposite to what God requires of us; to the extent that if God told us not to think about heaven, we would turn around and think about it just to spite Him, says Baxter.

Christian, are you so full of joy that you can't take any more? Are you claiming that by not thinking seriously, solemnly and frequently on heaven, you already have enough joy? Is there nothing in heaven that has no joy for you? If you only knew the joy that awaits you upon meditating solidly on heaven! *If you obeyed God, gave meditation a try, managed it every day, guarded your mind so that you gave it your complete and undivided attention, you would find yourself 'in the suburbs of heaven'.* Since God has His heart set on you, it is more reasonable for you to have your heart set on Him and think of the Father and your home.

That wretched nature of ours! We know what's best, we know the way to joy, and yet few of us love the way of joy in the sense of using the means by which we can possess it. 'Here is the misery of man's nature: Although every man naturally hates sorrow and loves the most happy and joyful life, yet few love the way to joy, or will endure the pains by which it is obtained.'

It is not enough to know about meditation. We may know more about it than many others. We must love meditation. Once we love meditation, that is, practise it so we discover its joy, the results will be evident. Once we get the taste of it, we will not want to stop meditation; rather like giving children lollies to eat – once the children taste them, you cannot persuade them to part with their lollies. More importantly, once you taste the sweetness of meditation, it will take away the strong resistance of sin. God designed this to be so, and that is why God went to much trouble, as it were, to tell us in His Word about the joys there will be in heaven. He tells us about the joys to come so that we will have joy in thinking about the joy to come. As a believer you know heaven will be wonderful, you know that the best Christians must be those who think about heaven frequently, so why not taste the sweetness of meditation for yourself? Just as you think upon the things of the world, with all its worthless and trivial ideas, think on heaven as much and soon your heart will be in heaven. Also, ensure that whenever you meet with other Christians, talk about heaven and how one gets there before you go your different ways in the world.

Every Christian knows it is his duty to ponder on our

everlasting rest, but few do it. They may become annoyed if they miss out on a sermon or public prayer, but it does not trouble them to miss out on meditation. It is essential as food is to the body. Digestion of God's Word 'turns the truths received and remembered into warm affection, firm resolution and holy conversation'. 'That which makes us most happy when we possess it, will make us most happy when we meditate on it.' *To do otherwise sets up a 'shyness' between you and God. To practise meditation does away with the shyness.*

Frequent meditation, Baxter suggests for himself, is best done in the evening, in the early part, from sunset to twilight.

Frequent meditation it must be. The Puritan not only has in mind deep thinking that will get us into heaven before we go to heaven, but that kind of deep thinking that makes us think twice before we sin. He claims that it is common to sin when the things of God pass through the mind rather quickly, but if those same things of God are considered seriously and form strong impressions on the mind through frequent pondering, then we shall sin far less frequently. Believers are 'uncomfortable' when they do not meditate as they should, when they let reason and faith go to sleep and do not stir themselves up to meditation. They know their meditation ought to be long and frequent if it is to be of any benefit, just as a man who feels cold may run a few steps to get warm, but it is not as effectual as running or walking for an hour. Until a believer practises meditation properly and exercises his mind at length, he will be uncomfortable; as 'a sudden and occasional thought of heaven will not raise our spiritual affections to any heat, yet meditation can continue our thoughts till our hearts grow warm'.

If we knew the return of Christ was only a few days off, or we knew that in a few days we would soon be in heaven, we would be full of emotion and longing! Well, the time for heaven may be some time away, but it is true that while here on earth the one that studies and ponders on heaven – the one who 'runs familiarly through the streets of Jerusalem, visiting the patriarchs and the prophets, saluting the apostles and admiring the army of martyrs' – is the one that 'firmly believes there is such a glory'.

What is meditation? It is preaching to one's self. It is entering into serious debate with your heart. Since the vile nature rears its ugly head even among the most devoted believers, there is the necessity of preaching against the vile nature as well as seriously debating against it in meditation. The spiritual man does well, for while 'the objects of faith are far off ', 'those of sense are nigh'. Through meditation we develop feelings through the power of our mind for heavenly things. This makes possible an awareness of that which we have never seen. Feelings have been our enemies for the cause of sin, but they become our friends when we employ them as instruments to reach for God. Indeed, God has given us feelings for this purpose. Otherwise, 'Why doth the Holy Spirit describe the glory of the new Jerusalem in expressions that are even grateful to the flesh?'

When does meditation become effective? We must always remember that our heart will not jump at the chance to meditate. Meditation is hard work. Even if you are convinced in your heart that thinking of this kind is good and will benefit you beyond measure; it does not mean your heart will automatically move on to meditating. You need to move your heart. For while your heart 'has nothing against the work', that is, it has no objections to it, it will deceive you. How will it deceive you? It will tell you to meditate some other time – maybe tomorrow, or the next day – and thus 'keep putting off the business'. You need to deal with your heart then: you need to persuade it to be up and meditating. 'Take no denial, chide it for its backwardness, use violence with it.' Then, when you begin studying and pondering the things of

God, make sure you do not stop meditating before it becomes effective. Stay long enough in it for it to have its effect. The heart can deceive you in this matter. So make sure you stay in meditation until you speak to God. 'Wilt thou go before thou hast seen Him?'

What happens if we do not meditate? Some will say that it is not worth the time and trouble to do it. *Yet, if we neglect it, it will dampen or destroy our love for God. It will make it unpleasant to think about God. It will pervert the judgment of God's ways. It will leave us open to sin so that we view sin as a pleasure. It will leave us fragile before trials and temptations of every kind.* In short, it will lead to a falling away from God. Take this warning: If you are unwilling to meditate as you should, then know that when you are dying and you are seeking comfort, you will have to find it from elsewhere. You were once advised on how you could attain joy and assurance, such as would carry through death, and last for eternity, but you refused.

Richard Baxter hoped that *The Saints' Everlasting Rest* would not merely give his readers an insight into the fruit of his studies of the subject, but through the reading of the book he hoped people could hear the breathing of his active hope and love.

His monumental work on meditation is such because it is in the spirit of the Word of God itself. The writer of Psalm 1 tells us to fix our delight and our desire in the law of the Lord with a view to our future destiny. The Psalmist implies that not only does the pondering of the Lord's law keep us from sin in regard to our present conduct, but it keeps our mind on only where there is true and final rest – or, in the words of Psalm 1, 'in the congregation of the righteous'. Note that even though the writer of Psalm 1 did not possess the knowledge of the eternal as we have it in the New Testament, his song is much occupied with our future destinies. And the rest of the Psalms, of which this one is an introduction, speak often of the future life as well.

Sometimes it is stated that the Old Testament dispensation was the age in which men, both good and bad, received their just deserts in this life, and life after death seemed to be only a shadowy concept for those who lived before Christ. A student of the Old Testament, however, cannot escape the thought that the righteous of the Old Testament dispensation were most conscious of not receiving what was promised (Hebrews 11:39). Those righteous who did not suffer much persecution and enjoyed some of the outward prosperity their brothers did not (Hebrews 11:33), in a sense gained what was promised, but did not receive what was promised in terms of future bliss.

All the godly were conscious that their rewards were not limited to this life only. Christ gave us the certain hope of the resurrection of the body through His own resurrection, but those of old knew a little of the future bliss of the soul as well. As Calvin says with respect to Psalm 1:4: '...we must look higher (than this life) if we desire to behold the assembly of the righteous'. Baxter has us considering that future assembly. To him it is beautiful to behold. In his meditations the great Puritan, Baxter, often imagined walking the streets of Jerusalem, greeting the prophets and the patriarchs, saluting the apostles and admiring the army of martyrs. His heart grew immensely warm in contemplation. Just as the author of Psalm 1 was occupied with thoughts of the future of the godly and the ungodly in the afterlife, so was Richard Baxter.

Who would not say the pastor of Kidderminster was not blessed? Yet all we who venture out to think as he did will be blessed and envied too.

3

JOHN FLAVEL

John Flavel (1630?–1691) was a Puritan as well. Like Richard Baxter he began as a Church of England minister, but, because of the Act of Uniformity in 1662, he was ejected from the Church of England and became a Nonconformist minister, a minister 'on the run'. He, like 2,000 other Puritan ministers in 1662, stood against what he regarded as a compromise with Rome, believing that we should only practise in the church that which is found in the Word of God.

The Act of Uniformity, and the subsequent acts brought in to quash Puritanism, made life very difficult for those who would not conform to the national religion. Heavy fines, imprisonment, transportation and exile threatened those believers who held secret meetings. It is believed 5,000 died from their sufferings in the years of trial that followed. Flavel had to leave his home and congregation in 1662 in Dartmouth. He first preached beyond the five mile restriction imposed on the ejected Puritans by going to a place called Slapton, the prescribed distance from Dartmouth. Many people of his congregation followed him to Slapton. He remained at Slapton until 1672, when King Charles II brought in the Declaration of Indulgence, giving the Puritans liberty to worship their own way. Even though the Indulgence was withdrawn, John Flavel continued to preach at Dartmouth, where he had returned in 1672. At great risk he preached in private homes, in forests, and even held meetings at low water on a rock in the Kingsbridge Estuary.

When persecution forced him to flee Dartmouth and he went

to London, he was fortunate to escape arrest; but he lived to enjoy the future liberties that were finally given to the Puritans. Most of Flavel's works – and he wrote many – were written in the times of persecution.

John Flavel was a great man of God. He suffered 35 years of great trial but he remained faithful to his Lord, with a longing to see unbelieving people converted and with a burning desire to see God's people united. He preached powerfully. One remarkable example of the effect of his preaching is told in the story of a hundred-year-old man who had gone to America to live, and who had heard Flavel preach in England eighty-five years before. He was suddenly arrested by the Spirit of God to recall Flavel's sermon of years ago and became converted at the horror of dying under the curse of God. There are other graphic examples of his influential ministry that one could draw on. It is said he had more followers in his time than Richard Baxter.

Flavel wrote some memorable works that show he knew the importance of believers thinking deeply on God's ways. Among those memorable works are *The Mystery of Providence* and *Keeping the Heart*.

The Mystery of Providence was written in a time of persecution when Flavel felt keenly the evilness of the world and the wickedness of sinners. In the spirit of the writer of Psalm 1, he is concerned with the preservation of God's people from evil and he devotes one of three parts of *The Mystery of Providence* to meditation itself. As the title of his book suggests, Flavel has in view the matter of the providence of God, defining providence in a somewhat quaint way. 'That there is a wise Spirit sitting in all the wheels of motion, and governing the most eccentric creatures and their most pernicious designs to blessed and happy issues.' In modern terms, the Puritan is saying we have a wise God who has control over all things, even over the most evil intents of wicked people, to order things for the happiness of his saints. It is interesting that *The Mystery of Providence* is based on Psalm 57:2, which concerns itself with David hiding from Saul in a cave. Flavel shows that David earnestly sought God in his extremity and that David recalls past experiences of God's help as an argument to encourage hope. It cannot be emphasized enough: deep reflection on the things of God often arise out of difficulties and troubles. From Flavel's hardships and David's trials we see the efforts made to reflect on 'former experiences' in *The Mystery of Providence,* that is, on what God has done for us in the past.

Here we have reflection on the law of the Lord in a sense other than that evidenced in *The Saints' Everlasting Rest. Baxter's work has us thinking on the future, while Flavel causes us to reflect more on the past and present.* Both are valid and essential in terms of meditation, and both see reflection as having to do with delighting and desiring in the law of the Lord and in meditating. One contemplates the ultimate, final and eternal division that will occur between the godly and the unrighteous, the other contemplates the working out of that division here in the present life as God begins, even from birth, and quite often well before the believer is actually converted, to do that which leads to conversion and beyond. So, Flavel gets us thinking about our birth, our upbringing, then our conversion in line with the truth that God in His sovereignty worked everything towards the time we came to know Him for our salvation.

Flavel bids us reflect on the remarkableness of our conversion. He writes: 'This, oh this, is the most excellent benefit you ever received [from Providence's hand]. You are more indebted to it for this, than for all your other mercies. And in explaining this performance of Providence, I cannot but think your hearts must be deeply effected. This is a subject which every gracious heart loves to steep its thoughts in. It is certainly the sweetest history that ever they repeated; they love to think and talk about it.' Lest some may be discouraged because their conversion was not as dramatic as others and may have had a conversion 'more obscure than confused', Flavel encourages them by reminding such converts that they can still remember God giving them a love for His people, a concern for sin, and so on. And all of us can recollect even the minutest circumstances that brought about such a wonderful change, the change that had to overcome the greatest difficulties. Flavel alludes to Paul's words in Ephesians, where it is stated that the power to raise us to new life after being dead in transgressions and sins is like the power the Father employed to raise Christ from the dead. This marvellous power springs from God's mercy and therefore recollection of it in terms of our salvation ought to occupy our mind frequently.

The *Mystery of Providence* goes on to consider our employment, our family affairs, our preservation from evil and the work of sanctification.

In regard to employment, it must not be regarded as mundane, unspiritual; it has to do with our well-being both here and in the world to come. The phrase 'the Puritan work ethic', which in modern times suggests that men are creatures designed only for work and not for leisure at all, is really complimentary to Puritans such as Flavel, as it reflects the high honour they accorded everyday work. It is not right to accuse the Puritans of frowning on leisure. In the chapter *On Employment* Flavel shows that differing circumstances, in regard to work, call for various responses to the working out of Providence. If one has a job that leaves little room for ease and rest, then he ought to thank God, as more ease and rest might have meant one has such temptations that lead to serving the devil in idleness. (This is the outlook that has given currency to the notion that the Puritans eschewed leisure.) Yet, if one has a job that leaves room for ease and rest, then he too ought to thank God, except he thanks God that the extra time allows for 'more time for heavenly exercises'.

Leisure for the Puritans meant opportunity to do spiritual things other than everyday work. Of course, the world has a different notion of leisure – no wonder it caricatures the Puritan. Well, whether one has much leisure or not, work as seen by Flavel is the means by which one can eat his own bread, provide necessities for the family, and provide for 'a surplus of works of mercy to others'. Work is not seen to be the be-all and end-all of a man's life to the extent that earning money becomes the sole object of life. Seneca is quoted in this context: 'I do not give, but lend myself to business.'

As for family affairs, our preservation from evil and the work of sanctification – other parts of our life wherein we ought to read Providence – there are many things for which to praise God, things that ought to be considered in the light of the hedge that God has fenced us in with against sin. In circumstances of many kinds we wish to break through the hedge. Providence exercises a control to ensure we are prevented from sinning by working externally on us, in conjunction with the Holy Spirit who is working internally in us.

The Work of Providence

Because God works for our good in Providence, we have a duty to meditate on how Providence works for us. Unless we meditate, Flavel contends:

(a) we shall not praise God for the good things He has done for us;

(b) we shall lose sight of the benefits He has given us;

(c) we shall be found slighting God when we do not take notice of what good He is doing;

(d) we cannot pray intelligently unless we are aware of our circumstances as moulded by Providence.

How do we meditate on Providence? There are five main directions that John Flavel gives us:

Firstly, we should think through what God has done from first to last in a complete way, going back as far as we can to all the evidences of His Providence.

Secondly, we should relate the evidence of Providence with the Word of God and all it says by way of threats, cautions, counsel and promises – in this way we see Scripture to be true.

Thirdly, we are to make sure that we see God as the one who orders all the events of our lives, the bitter and the sweet.

Fourthly, we ought to be moved considerably in our feelings for the particular things that occur through Providence, sorrowing if we need to sorrow but being joyful for the most part, as there is no reason whatever at any time to give up our essential joy.

Fifthly and lastly, we should see that we do not grow sad and become impatient if there is ever any delay in God's blessing coming our way.

What are the advantages of meditating on Providence? Many in every way. *Through meditating on God's Providence we shall gladly communicate with God – the mercies of God become 'fuel to maintain a good man's love to God'*. Through it we shall take great pleasure in observing how harmonious the ways of God are for us, even though sometimes His ways may contradict one another until we see them all running together. Through such meditation we shall overcome 'the natural atheism' that is in our hearts. Through it we shall gain a significant support for our faith in future exigencies. Praise and thanksgiving will rise up from our hearts as we remember past blessings, and praise and thanksgiving is 'the sweetest part of our lives'. Jesus Christ will become dearer to us each day.

Take note of Providence and your heart will melt in submission before the Lord, who will bring tranquillity to the mind in times of any convulsive changes. This adds to improving holiness within. And when the hour of death comes, a study of Providence will be of singular benefit, as the time of death is usually when Satan is at his worst with all kinds of evil suggestions. If we have been accustomed to treasuring up the memories of Providence before our dying day, then our souls 'will not give up so easily a truth which ... has so often been felt and tasted'. The first and last acts of faith are the two most momentous acts of faith. The first one was when we 'initially threw ourselves upon Christ'; and the last one is 'a great venture too' when it casts itself 'into the ocean of eternity upon the belief of a promise'.

After he has considered Providence in the light of meditation, this Puritan of Dartmouth has another significant contribution to help us remember the ways of God for our own benefit and for others. What is the useful thing to do? Keep a diary or a journal of what God is doing in your life. If more believers did this, the Church of God would be enriched more. The Church would greatly benefit if Christians, who had both the time and the ability to keep a written record, did so.

A written record need not disclose all that a Christian experiences – 'religion does not lay all open' – but there is room for prudent, humble and timely observations.

A written record in its usefulness will comprise passages of Scripture that have impressed, together with events that fall out in our own time and experience. This will become an antidote 'against the spreading atheism of these days' and convince us that the Lord is God. All too frequently we look at events as natural causes, or fail to see them in the light of their spiritual significance – this is what Flavel has in mind when he refers to 'atheism'. So many of us fail in this respect. We must arrest the spreading atheism and prevent the contagion from tainting us, and a regular diary makes us conscious of the need to do this.

Our memories are 'slippery'. Things that make a vivid impression on our mind may not be easily forgotten, yet it is not uncommon for new impressions to crowd out old ones. We cannot rely on our memory, and a written record of Providence will ensure that we keep a permanent reminder of all that has taken place. Besides, our diaries or journals shall become useful to others. Just as we cannot take our money with us, so when we die we cannot take our diaries or journals – but, like riches, our records benefit those to whom we leave them. Indeed, to leave behind a literary account of God's dealings with you in this life is a greater treasure than any money, house, or whatever material you bequeath.

Yet there is more to writing out from day to day the things of Providence. There is also the benefit you gain, whenever you have new needs or difficulties, in going back over your diaries or journals and reminding yourself of the way God has spoken to you in the past. As Asaph did (Psalm 77:5), you can reflect on the days of old. Was I ever distressed before? How did God help me out before? Remember that even though the present trial seems like the greatest one you have ever faced and you are tempted to believe nothing like this has ever happened before, those former trials were just as great and your fear then was just as intense. Do not look down on what happened in the past. Look at your old records. Preserve your memory against the present fear. 'Make it as much your business to preserve the sense and value as the memory of former providences, and the fruit will be sweet to you.'

The Mystery of Providence, as one can see, blends in beautifully with *The Saints' Everlasting Rest*. One looks at the future, the other looks at the past and the present, and through them both we find the balance that one needs to appreciate all that God is doing for us. We are exhorted to delight in and desire God's Word, to meditate on it day and night. What outlook should we have as we meditate? As it has already been stated before, the outlook includes a consideration of the truths that there are only two kinds of people in the world and that their destinies greatly differ, the godly congregating together in eternal felicity with their Jehovah-God, and the wicked perishing in their disobedience. Yet our outlook is also to include the truth that on the way to the Final and the Ultimate the godly prospers. The godly is described as a well-watered, fruitful tree, with the result that 'Whatever he does prospers'.

As believers we may baulk at such a thought of the godly prospering in this life, particularly if our life has known many trials and troubles. We may think that events in our lives seem to fit no good or divine purpose, yet there is Providence, a present working for the good of all those who have been called by God. The words of Psalm 1:3 more fully mean 'Whatever he does prospers and comes to maturity'. As Flavel says, the ways of Providence may cross over and contradict one another, but there comes a time when all God's ways come running together. It may even be that they do not run together completely in this life for some dear children of God, but we are assured that they will according to His Word. God's Providence can be quite complex really, and there can be even an interplay of events other than our own in terms of God's ways – other people's lives may crisscross with ours, and what appears to be a loss for one person may be a gain for another. For instance, how many times have we heard about the death of one person leading to the conversion of another? I have heard of a lovely Christian lady dying and her death led to the conversion of her unbelieving husband. The wife died and it appeared to be a great loss, yet it is certain she in the glory to come will see her immature death in terms of prosperity, as her husband will be there too with inexpressible happiness. Her loss, his gain? No, gain for both of them. How strange but how wonderful are the ways of God! Everything, yes, everything the godly does, prospers, even in this life, even up to and including what occurs in death itself.

All these things require much meditation. If a believer understands meditation correctly, he will be overwhelmed by the wealth of things to think about. He shall understand that life is not only meditation, but he will realise that he could well spend all his life just meditating. Just think of all the pages of God's Word, think of the study one can do of all the things that have happened in one's life, think what can be pondered on in regard to what God has also planned for us. Why, the thoughts on such things are potentially countless! Of course, it is not possible to tread the ground of all that we could reflect on, yet may we not be guilty of passing through only a little when our Jehovah-God has given us so much land and forest to enjoy?

Things of the Heart

Keeping the Heart, Flavel's other great work under consideration, is based on Proverbs 4:23 and was written out of the conviction that while God's children have a new heart in Christ upon being converted, the new heart is like a musical stringed instrument which, though it was once tuned exactly, can become out of tune easily. The heart of the Christian needs to be kept 'tuned'.

Flavel suggests six things that are necessary in order to make possible the keeping of the heart:

Firstly, he writes that we should converse with our hearts.

'There are some people who have lived forty or fifty years in the world, and have had scarcely one hour's discourse with their own hearts.' Such people are, as another Puritan Thomas Watson put it, 'very good at foreign policy but a stranger in their own country'. Even the heathen could say, 'The soul is made wise by sitting still in quietness.'

Secondly, Flavel says the heart is kept humble over the evils in the heart.

Thirdly, prayer ought to be sent up for grace.

Fourthly, there should be a strong resolve to walk more carefully with God.

Fifthly, a jealousy must be kept for holiness and a fear lest sin quickly breaks out.

Lastly, an awareness of God's omniscience needs to be realized to keep the heart from sin.

While John Flavel admits keeping the heart is a very difficult thing to do, yet because it is a constant thing which needs to be done, he regards it as the most important business of a Christian's life. Why is it important?

It is important because it concerns itself with the glory of God. This in turn sets us thinking about how sincere we are in our walk with God, taking care that we are not hypocrites. To avoid being hypocrites, we must oppose sins 'in their first rise', that is, as soon as they come into our mind. The attractiveness of a Christian's walk springs from what takes place in the heart. Christians can never convince the world until 'they apply again to heart-work'. Besides, the believer feels more comfortable when he is no stranger to what is going on in his mind and is accustomed to reflecting deeply on his conduct. He knows his assurance of salvation comes from keeping the heart.

True, the Holy Spirit assures us, but we also gain assurance by taking 'pains with (our) own hearts'. Flavel tells of a man who sought assurance through some extraordinary sign from heaven, but eventually found assurance when he began to search the Word of God as well as looking at his own heart. Another man is quoted as being stilled after being shaken by temptation, once he subjected his understanding to the Scriptures and compared his heart with them. Yes, the Spirit witnesses to us objectively, but in our hearts we must apply ourselves to discerning the way the Spirit comes to us – without serious searching and diligent watching of the heart Flavel cannot imagine how the workings of the Spirit can be discerned. The Holy Spirit shines with grace in our heart when He not only 'infuses the grace', but also opens our eyes as well through the sincerity we have. This assurance is not usually given to lazy believers. A careless Christian may have assurance for a time, but he will not have it for long. 'I never knew grace to thrive in a careless soul.' What is more, the power of temptation is broken through watching the heart, particularly when the first suggestions of sin creep in or assault the mind.

Strictly speaking, the rest of *Keeping the Heart* is not occupied with meditation – being occupied with the heart facing its severest tests – but the ten motives, which appear at the end of this rather little work for exhorting us to keep the heart, need to be studied. This does not mean Flavel's observations about the heart's severest tests are not worth reading – far from it – but to keep more strictly to the subject of meditation we now turn to the motives Flavel puts forward as necessary for studying, observing and diligently keeping the heart. What are the motives?

He tells us that examining the heart will help us understand 'the deep mysteries of religion'. He who examines his heart will find the Scriptures make sense, for what one reads in the Scriptures will reflect much on what the honest meditator experiences. This in turn will secure the heart against any dangerous errors that are around. For why do so many depart from the faith? Is it not because they never knew what led to practical godliness? That is, they never knew that keeping the heart is the safest means of remaining secure.

If you keep your heart, you will prove to be sincere. It is true that hypocrites may go to great lengths and do many religious outward acts, but if they have not kept the heart, then all their acts are a sham, yes, even their cry about their own wickedness on their deathbed. You see, a man will say anything to get relief if he is on the rack and being tortured, and a hypocrite will cry out in difficulty to get relief, but he is not sincere. The fact that you take so much care and diligence to keep your heart before difficulty proves you are sincere – you are obviously doing it not for show, to be seen by men.

If you keep your heart, then praying, hearing sermons and the like, are a joy to you, whereas they have little joy for him who has not been faithful in looking at his heart. Some almost go through their prayers, or almost hear the whole sermon, before they become interested in the things of God, but if you keep your heart, you are the first to 'get sight of Christ in a sermon', you are first to see Christ in the Lord's Supper or baptism, you are the first to taste the grace and love of God in secret prayer. Some are hardly any better off by doing those things a believer should do, but in keeping the heart such things will prove to be of great comfort and profit to you.

If you keep your heart, you will never run short of matters to pray over. Not only will you not run short of things to say, but you will know what to say, as well as being able to express clearly what you want to say.

Did you know too that if more believers kept their heart, we would stand a better hope of seeing revival, which is 'the most desirable thing in the world'. At the present time many who profess to be Christians are spiritually dead. Oh for the day when holiness shines through all that Christians say and do so that the world looks on in awe and respects the gospel! When will such a time be? Only when believers take to examining their heart and thinking deeply on the things of God. Are you grieved that we are not experiencing revival, that the world ridicules and scorns us who believe? If you are grieved – grieved over your own heart as well as the hearts of other believers – 'recover your credit' and begin keeping your heart, says Flavel.

Others will easily stumble and fall, but you will not if you keep your heart faithfully. You will be ready for any situation. Nothing will perturb you. Like Paul, you will turn every kind of circumstance to your benefit.

If God's people all kept their hearts, we would also know of better fellowship with each other. If we all had better communion with the Father and the Son, we would with ease stir each other up spiritually. *If we spent more time and laboured more to examine our hearts and think on spiritual truth, our lives would be so attractive that others could not help themselves from wanting to be in our company.* 'It is the pride, passion and earthiness of our hearts, that has spoilt Christian fellowship.' Christians meet and are disagreeable with each other. We are uncharitable towards each other because we do not know enough about ourselves. We are unfeeling because we ourselves do not feel – do not feel our weaknesses and tendencies towards temptation. We meet and say little of spiritual profit to one another, and it is because there is little of spiritual profit in ourselves. If as believers we all kept our hearts, 'the beauty and glory of communication would be restored'. We would fight less, criticize less. If we were more sensitive about how evil our hearts are, we would 'feel right one toward another'.

Lastly, if you keep your heart, your impression of spiritual truth will be more lasting that it is now. Realize that we are not talking about a small matter. Is it a small matter for your spiritual understanding to improve? Is it a small matter to make yourself safe and well-secured in the things of God? Is it a small matter to make your communion with God sweeter? A small thing to know the actual power of godliness? A small thing to have your doubts and misgivings removed? A small matter to become a better instrument to serve Christ? To know the communion of the saints as it used to be in the Early Church? To know the means of grace in an abiding way? If these matters are not small, then do that work to make these blessings yours. Keep the heart.

How do you keep the heart by way of habit? Be earnest about it. Make up your mind to give yourself to it – in all your understanding, your memory, your conscience and your feelings. Defend your heart with the Spirit's sword, the Word of God. Call yourself all the time to account; examine yourself in the presence of the All-seeing One; bring your conscience forward to the judgment of the Word. Take care that you guard yourself against the ways of the world. When there is the first slightest sign that you are moving away from a consciousness of God, when you first sense a lack of interest in meditation, watch out. Yet it is not all painful striving. If you keep your heart, you will find blessings flowing in on you. You will become excited and exhilarated, and you will wear your enemies down. Then heaven itself will be opened to you and the allotment promised to you will be yours, as it will be for all those who overcome.

Matters of Death
Mention must also be made about some of John Flavel's other observations as they come to us in such works as *Treatise of the Soul of Man*, *A Practical Treatise of Fear* and *The Causes and Cures of Mental Errors*.

In Flavel's *Treatise of the Soul of Man*, he argues that we ought to think about death, particularly our own death before it comes. To do this, firstly we must shed our mind of those cares and thoughts that are unnecessary, rather like the captain of a ship that is simply crossing over the English Channel and who does not need to carry as much as he needs if he were bound for the West Indies. 'Most men's provisions, at least their cares and their thoughts, are far beyond the preparations of their abode in this world.' We must occupy ourselves mainly with what is necessary to live as we hope to live soon – if we are sure we are bound for heaven, we ought to live as one bound for heaven soon. We should begin to be what we expect to be, realizing that there is nothing between us and those who have died – only a puff of breath, a space of time. Careful thinking along these lines causes thoughts of our own death to spring vividly before us.

Some may think that because every believer is said in Scripture to be equally free of the sting and the curse of death, there will be no fear of death for any believer when it comes, but this is not so. Flavel says that not every child of God is equally favoured in being spared of the agonies and fear of death. Therefore, Christians must become accustomed to imagining their own death and bracing themselves for that end. It is like the old soldier who, unlike the new soldier, does not find battle anywhere near as frightening. Are you frightened as you think of your own death? At first it may scare you, but the more you meditate on it, the less frightening it will be. Men tame a young colt by riding it up to what scares it the most, but, upon smelling what scares it, the young colt is cured of its fear.

We should not fear our separation from this life. In thinking of our own death, we must meditate too on the truth that heaven is as ready and fit to receive us as it will ever be, that Scripture tells us this is so, that reason tells us it is true as well. Already the guilt of our sin has been done away with through our justification. The filth of our sin is being removed by sanctification. Our tendency to sin will be totally eradicated when we are glorified in the future. Even the regret, the reluctancy and the sadness of the soul in parting at the end argues strongly for the belief that it longs to be reunited with the body again. Our love for Christ and the things above does not rob us of our love for the body. True, love for Christ and the things above conquer and subdue the body, but the soul's longing to be with the body is always there.

Now, when death itself comes upon us, our previous meditation on it does much to help us, even though in death we are not as rational as before. Death brings many 'disturbances and frequent interruptions' so that we are not fully in our right mind, and all that we wish to do for ourselves then will only be done in short bursts of normal rationality. Those watching us die can do little to help us very often, as there are too few who have the wisdom, the experience and the faithfulness to the gospel to help. We are on our own. Previous meditation can aid us in that dark hour, if we have brought ourselves to the state of being willing to die. How do we bring ourselves to die? By becoming acquainted with death. How do we become acquainted with it? By accustoming ourselves to thinking 'assiduously and calmly of it'.

What are some thoughts that may help us to face death calmly? Surely, we must think of Jesus. Now, in this life there are degrees of assurance, and some have barely assurance at all – some have thrown themselves on Christ for mercy without receiving the assurance of being accepted – but anyone who dies in Christ will go to heaven. It does not matter how much assurance one has, it does not make him any 'safer'. He who has no or little assurance goes to heaven just as well. This is not stated to promote indifference about assurance, but simply to comfort all believers at their death, when they may not be confident at such a dark hour about their status in Christ. Still, all believers receive foretastes of heaven of some kind while here on earth, and in our contemplation of death the memory of such foretastes can encourage us to face the end more nobly. The foretastes that we have experienced ought to create a longing in us to be rid of our body, 'to venture through death itself for the full enjoyment of those delights and pleasures'. We must all die, but such preparation can 'sweeten' what can be a bitter time.

Some Christians may not want to die because they are not perfect enough yet or because they feel God wants them to remain here for further service. If you think you are not perfect enough to die and you are burdened by existing sin that you think you could overcome if given more time, you should realize that it does not matter how long you were alive, there would always be some sin you had not overcome. As long as we are alive here on earth, we will be in sin. And if you employ the argument that you are not ready to die yet because of sin you want to overcome, you would never be ready to die. You may be concerned about serving God for better and further service, but besides God's work not needing the help of man, remember that God has a higher and a more excellent service for you in heaven, where you will do much more than you could have ever done on earth.

Regarding the certainty of hell
Even though John Flavel probably has unbelievers in mind when he writes of hell – it is surprising how many unbelievers were converted in Puritan days through reading books or works that were essentially for Christians – believers ought to consider hell as well as heaven, according to the way the Puritan perceives it in *Treatise of the Soul of Man*. Thoughts of hell will make one more aware of the horrifying end for sinners, as well as making one far more conscious of the purpose of man's existence. Flavel quotes a heathen as saying: 'I am greater and born to greater

things than I should be a slave to my body.' Many people think too much about what to drink, what to eat and what to put on, when every thought spent on bodily needs a thousand thoughts spent on the question 'What shall I do to be saved?' The torments of hell are endless, never exceeding the demerits of sin – for sin is evil against the absolute perfect being of God. No description is adequate for the torments of hell. No man can imagine how terrible they are. Therefore, 'there can never be too much care, too much study or pains about that which can never be too well secured.' Both believers and unbelievers underestimate the seriousness of being prepared for eternity. If they were more aware of the seriousness of being prepared, they would spend more time, more thoughts and more prayers 'to make these things sure'.

Irrational fear

Assurance comes to the fore in Flavel's *A Practical Treatise of Fear*. Flavel makes the acute observation that the cruelest torment on earth is that which we give ourselves. *The cruelest torment? Our own fears. 'Some fear more than they ought, and some before they ought, and others when they ought not at all.'* We may decry that our faith is too weak, but really our fears are too strong. What is a cure for fear? Think, reflect in the heart about all the calamities and miseries mankind brings down on itself by its sinful fears. Think on this in terms of both this world and the world to come. We in this modern world should actually have less to fear because many believers have gone before us enduring what were for them 'strange and untried torments'; therefore we today are fighting an enemy whom we know has been defeated before time and again. As Christians we ought to take heart and dispel our fears in thinking of those past triumphs and set ourselves to gaining assurance. This assurance ought to be of the kind that 'overawes [our] hearts everyday, and in every place with the eye of God'.

Avoidance of Error

Meditation also comes within the confines of the defence of the truth against false teaching and error. *Meditation embraces the ability to reflect on truth, being able to distinguish it calmly from error, as well as being able to differentiate between what is scriptural and what is sheer opinion.* Flavel considers such reflection in his quaintly-titled *The Causes and Cure of Mental Errors.*

Opinion must always be distinguished from 'matters of faith', from matters of doctrinal teaching as verified by the Word of God. Flavel contends that we should be ready to dispense with opinion and give it up to truth if need be, whereas 'matters of faith' are those things for which one ought to be prepared to die. For Flavel, opinions can be either 'matters of faith' (and things that grow to be matters of faith when it is realized that they are correct teachings) or 'errors'. Since errors have a sly and seemingly modest way of creeping into the church, while often the supporters of truth are not always good at defending it, Flavel spends much time in *The Causes and Cures of Mental Errors* exposing the danger of error stealing in to the church, together with insistence on the need for believers to think contemplatively and rationally about error's attempts to put an end to truth.

The good Puritan realizes not all believers are capable of refuting evil, but he offers counsel for those who are. There are believers who love the truth, are prepared to die for it, but they cannot dispute for it. So his counsel is for those whose ability and prudence matches their zeal and love. Flavel counsels that such men ought not to cure the church of error by compulsion or external force, but 'by rational conviction and proper spiritual remedies'. Note 'rational conviction'. This 'rational conviction' comes through being acquainted with the reason why errors arise, with a study of the reason 'within and without', involving a study of the way errors develop amongst people and within people. There are rules for the prevention and cure of error, but before the application of such rules is carried out, the supporters of the truth must encourage believers to read the Scriptures in order to form correct conclusions. This does not mean all believers have the right to expound publicly and preach the Word to others, but it means all have the right to discuss privately and edify each other.

Error often arises, however, when all believers, or many believers, are given the right to expound publicly. God has not given such a gift to all. Christians who do not have a public ministry ought to note that Christ Himself has put limitations on the Church; but they are free to examine the Word in order to see for themselves where any error lies, the error to which those of the public ministry are pointing.

Error is brought in by crafty ways, therefore there is a need for some careful thinking to be done. *Error often comes dressed in 'new notions, and new modes of language, method, tone and gesture', so that it appears as a notion that has not been considered before, making the perpetrator of the error appear as an original thinker and one who is superior to those who have gone before him.* Error also comes as 'too importunate and pressing upon you', that is, it gives or demands little time to think. As an antidote to all this, the supporter of the truth needs to reflect slowly and surely, knowing God's Word will refer to the newfangled erroneous teaching somewhere on its pages, and that the truth which the error threatens to destroy will emerge triumphantly as the truth of today, just as it was the truth of yesteryear.

Exposing error is not an easy task, and it cannot be emphasised enough: only careful observation of any error through serious and deep, contemplative thinking will see through the folly and note the fruit of it. Flavel in his wisdom makes us vividly aware of the importance of not being hasty in this matter. The following pregnant sentence ought to be written and framed on the wall of the study of every man of God: 'Indeed we must not make those errors that are none; nor stretch any innocent expression to that purpose; nor yet be too hasty in meddling in contention till we cannot be silent and innocent; and then, whatever the expense be, truth will repay it.'

One can see that John Flavel, more than Richard Baxter, took in a greater panorama of subject matter suitable for meditation, if one relies on their works for their evidence. *Flavel considers meditation in relation to Providence, meditation in relation to keeping our heart by relying on 'former experiences', meditation with regard to the importance of the soul in the light of eternity, meditation with respect to the fight against fear, and meditation in relation to the defence of the truth against error.* The thoughts of Flavel accord well with the Word of God: the godly man is like a well-watered tree. To change the metaphor, the godly man is ever looking back and looking forward to note that everything is bringing about his prosperity, that even death is not to be feared since death will make possible his entry into the congregation of the godly, which congregation the wicked will not join because in their earthly life they spent their lives in the irrational fear of men and in the morbid occupation of pursuing that which counts for little. One suspects that Flavel's view of meditation was greatly sharpened by the persecution he suffered, and that he knew from the heart what he once wrote: '...an assured Christian was never known to be a coward in sufferings'. No craven Christian could write that, but neither could an unthinking Christian.

4

JOHN BUNYAN

John Bunyan (1628–1688) was a Puritan writer and preacher. Like his father he was both a maker and mender of utensils. He received little education, but whatever grasp of the English language he acquired in his early years probably came from reading the Bible. Still, as a youngster he cared little for the Bible. He later wrote: 'the Scriptures thought I, what are they? ... Give me a ballad, a newsbook, George on horseback; give me some book that teaches curious arts, that tells of old fables; but for the Holy Scriptures I cared not.'

When John Bunyan was fifteen, his mother and sister died within a month of each other. Later in that same year he left home and enrolled in the Parliamentary Army to play his part in the Civil War, which had been going for two years by then. He was a soldier for the Roundheads, opponents of the Royalist followers of King Charles I.

In 1648 he married a woman who had godly parents. As her dowry, she brought to Bunyan two books that convinced Bunyan he was a sinner who needed God's forgiveness to go to heaven. He attempted to reform himself, however, for God's approval, even giving up dancing and bell-ringing at the local parish church.

His conversion to God and his distrust in his own good works owes much to the day when in Bedford he overheard 'three or four poor women sitting at a door in the sun, and talking about the things of God'. Shortly after, Bunyan had a dream about the same women. In the dream he saw the poor women on the sunny side of a high mountain, while he was shivering and cut off from them by a wall in which he was searching for an opening. He found an opening but it was narrow. He tried again and again to get through it. At last he got his head through, then his shoulders, then his whole body. He joined the women in gladness in the sun.

His conversion amounted to a considerable time of travail of soul, as his classic *Grace Abounding to the Chief of Sinners* attests. After the dream about the women, the words of Luke 14:22 'And yet there is room', encouraged him to believe there was a place in heaven for him; yet there was a fear Christ would not call him. He then met John Clifford, the pastor of the Independent Church of Bedford, but after talking to Clifford, Bunyan felt even more discouraged. He envied the animals who did not have a sinful nature, until he heard a sermon of comfort for those who felt God was hiding His face from them: 'Thou art My love, and nothing shall separate thee from My love'. Bunyan felt a genuine peace of mind and called that time 'a true manifestation of grace to the soul'.

It appears Bunyan was genuinely converted at the time the sermon on the Song of Solomon 4:1 comforted him, but *Grace Abounding to the Chief of Sinners* shows us the Tempter was not ready to give up on losing Bunyan to the Saviour. For a long time the new convert was 'tossed between the Devil and his ignorance'.

One cannot help believe the Devil knew Bunyan would become a Christian of great influence, therefore he fought with more than usual power to wrest him from the arms of Christ. The Devil once said to Bunyan, 'Even if it takes me seven years to wear you down, I will do it'. Satan dreaded Bunyan's ultimate triumph over doubts and fears. The curious thing is that Bunyan was not melancholic in nature, and after his conversion and some years of satanic assaults he was not prone to dark despair and despondency again, but rather seemed full of assurance and hope until his dying day.

In 1653 Bunyan joined the three-year-old Independent Church of Bedford. Within two or three years of joining, he began to preach publicly as one of the 'mechanick preachers', scornfully looked down on by the regular and licensed clergy of the day, until such time he was arrested for preaching without a licence. Obviously, the tinker made an impact with his preaching and the 'indecent haste' to silence him led to his imprisonment in 1660. His imprisonment lasted intermittently from 1660 to 1672. In the early part of his internment he managed to get parole occasionally, but for the most part of those twelve years he suffered long separation and distress of being parted from his wife and poor children, especially his blind child.

In prison he spent his time making laces and writing. Much of his writing was the fruit of meditation in prison. Even after he was released in 1672 and had become pastor of the local church, a warrant was put out for his arrest in 1675, but it is not clear if it was put into effect. He was locked up once more in 1677, when during his six months' imprisonment he put the finishing touches to his famed work *Pilgrim's Progress*. During imprisonment it is said his pen was never idle. Certainly he was never idle in meditation. In his first imprisonment at least he only possessed the Bible and Foxe's *Book of Martyrs*, but he wrote prolifically, among his writings being *Profitable Meditations*, *I Will Pray with the Spirit*, *Christian Behaviour*, *Serious Meditations on the Four Last Things*, *The Holy City* and *Grace Abounding*.

In *Prison Meditations* he wrote:

> For though men keep my outer man
> Within their locks and bars
> Yet by the faith of Christ I can
> Mount higher than the stars.

> Their fetters cannot spirits tame,
> Nor tie up God from me;
> My faith and hope they cannot lame,
> Above them I shall be.

There is a beautiful occasion drawn well for us by Frank Mott Harrison, whose biography of John Bunyan is described by Rev. W. Y. Fullerton as that which 'will ever remain the standard book of reference in all that concerns the life and history of [Bunyan]'. The scene is the lock-up, the year is about 1665:

Bunyan, regarded by his fellow-prisoners as their chaplain, one day assembled with them for worship; and as he stands to address his brethren he is silent. Instead of the exhortation to which they were looking forward, he returns to his seat, and bows his head upon the open Bible upon his knees. The men look at each other and then at the preacher. John Bunyan gazes again and again at the printed page with sorrowful expression; but by degrees the shadowed brow lightens up, and, rising once more to his feet, and 'lifts up his eyes to Heaven', his features gleam with joy as he announces the text: 'Glorious things of Thee are spoken, O City of God' (Ps. 87:3) and another: 'And the name of that city from that day shall be, THE LORD IS THERE' (Ezek. 48:35). This sermon develops into his book called *The Holy City*, and in the preface he says: 'I thought I should not have been able to speak among them so much as five words of truth with life and evidence; but I with a few groans did carry my meditation to the Lord Jesus for a blessing, which He did forthwith grant according to His grace; and helping me to set it before my brethren, we did all eat and were refreshed.

Bunyan may not have always approached his preaching in the above manner, but it is safe to conclude that the great but lowly man was one who frequently took his thoughts to Jesus for a blessing first. The groaning was groaning in the Spirit, divine help was sought through Bunyan's inexpressible wish to relay from his heart to others the fruit of his thinking upon reading the Word. *He knew that while his meditations were rich to himself, only by the Spirit and through Jesus' blessing could those same meditations breathe with the same power among his hearers. What a lesson for all preachers!*

Bunyan's work *Profitable Meditations* was published in 1661 in the early part of his twelve-year internment. These meditations appeared in the form of a poem and arose out of Bunyan's burning desire to make his thoughts public through the printed page when the authority of the land had prevented him from preaching. So many who had or could not hear Bunyan, 'read these noiseless messengers of glad tidings in private'. The poem is divided into nine parts:

1. Of Man by Nature
2. Of the Sufferings of Christ
3. Of the Saints or Church
4. A Discourse between Satan and a tempted Soul
5. A Discourse between Christ and a Sinner
6. A Discourse between Christ and a doubting Soul
7. A Discourse between Death and a Sinner
8. A Discourse between Death and a Saint
9. A Discourse of the Day of Judgment, both with the Godly and the Ungodly.

After an introduction, John Bunyan in *Profitable Meditations* begins by expressing surprise that men cannot see the foolishness of following a life of sin since they know it must be attributed to blindness of heart. It is plain that men are blind for 'their hearts for Heav'n are cool'. If men only sensed the eternal consequences of their sin they would 'fly from sin'. Why don't they? Men run at the beck and call of Satan until at last they feel the flames of hell. Men are clever at searching out things of the world, but they shun what they well know about God, all because they do not 'feel the pain' for their sins. Men are clever, but they are fools and ought to wake up and lay to heart what the consequences of sin are and 'get heaven'.

What is the remedy for the sinner? He must meditate. He is not called on to make a rash, spur-of-the-moment decision and believe on Christ, (after the style of many who make quick decisions in modern day evangelism). No, he is to think on, ruminate and consider deeply the things of salvation in order to come to his senses.

He must think seriously on the sufferings of Christ. It is true that 'the pains He bore are more than we can think'; yet think on those pains he must – the pains of the Father hiding His face from Him, the pains of bearing our accursed sin. We as sinners sin without much care, we sin with pleasure, but our sin made Christ groan. We ought to consider this. Still, we ought to go on to consider that His love was such that through His sufferings He now has in possession heaven and earth and death and hell, to do with in whatever way He likes. This is good news for the believer, but it ought to bring fear on those who 'do not care for His blood to cleanse their hearts'. The sinner who believes has good reason to rejoice; since Christ is His, the Spirit of grace has been sent by the Father to his poor heart.

Does meditation continue to be a blessing once the sinner turns to Christ and is washed in Christ's precious blood? Not always, for Satan will not allow it to be so. Satan compels the believer to taste meditation of another kind, the kind that is designed to destroy the believer through doubt. Yet when Satan comes to tempt, what threatens to be a bitter and soul-destroying meditation can be the means of blessing if we stand our ground and answer him according to the truth of God's grace. Meditation can be soul-destroying in the sense that Satan loves to get the believer alone and throw accusations at him.

What exactly can the believer do when meditation threatens to undo all the good work the Spirit has done in the soul? Well, Satan will say we are too sinful to be saved, we are hypocritical, that there is no evidence we are saved, that evidence or blessing may be tasted and then one can fall away from salvation, that we are not one of the elect, that we shall not be able to hold out until the end, that he will pursue us to the end to undo us. So, what can the believer do? He can meet Satan face-to-face by answering him by both what the Scriptures teach and by the experience that has changed his heart, when he is able to declare:

> He that hath set His love upon me now.
> Will always keep me with His tender eye;
> Thou also know'st thine head (Satan's) hath He made bow.
> This is He in whose bosom I must lie.

It is true that *Profitable Meditations* included originally the long title 'Profitable Meditations, Fitted to Man's Different Condition: in a Conference between Christ and the Sinner in Nine Particulars', implying that all the discourses between Satan and the doubting soul were actually discourses between Satan and sinners. Yet one can see from the way that 'the tempted soul' of the fourth particular in the poem answers Satan, he is one who had not only tasted the heavenly love but had been rid of this guilt and pain of sin, God confirming 'more than once or twice' with His sweet promises. Therefore, Bunyan views him as a true believer, though Bunyan classes him as a sinner too (just as James in James 4:8 calls believers 'sinners'). In Bunyan's mind all men are sinners, only some are saved sinners, while many are unsaved sinners.

Obviously, the sinner of the fifth particular is different from the one of the fourth particular. The latter is he who believes truly but is tempted by Satan, while the former is one who, in the midst of a kind of enforced meditation, is confronted by Christ and seeks to delay believing in Him to be saved. He is the sinner who tells Christ he will believe some other time, who does not yet want to forsake the world, who wants sin to have his heart though he has 'a mind for heaven', who finds pleasure in sin, who bemoans losing his friends if he should believe, who thinks he will turn to Christ only when death comes, who has too much to do in the world to consider Jesus. One may say that all men meditate on spiritual things in their life, but there is an involuntary meditation when Christ presents His claims to those who do not want to hear but cannot help hearing. Still, a procrastinating sinner may read the words Bunyan penned, and they could become profitable for meditation if he saw the stupidity of rejecting Jesus.

The case of the sinner in the sixth particular is different again. He is described as a 'doubting soul' who in his meditation bewails his sinfulness and thinks he is too vile to be received by the Saviour. He is encouraged to believe he will be accepted because Jesus wants to make Himself a name by saving him. The sinner is required to 'Believe My word and meditate the same'. Through meditation and serious thinking he will climb out of despair – as he thinks of the Lord's past act of being wounded on the cross for him and the Lord's present act of making mention of the sinner's name through intercession in heaven.

Bunyan's view of Death

Two more subjects remain as matters for meditation according to Bunyan in his *Profitable Meditations*: that of death and the day of judgment.

With respect to death, Bunyan considers both death and the

sinner and death and the saint. Particulars Seven and Eight describe 'A Discourse between Death and a Sinner' and 'A Discourse between Death and a Saint'. What we may regard simply as thoughts on death by both sinner and saint, Bunyan views as 'discourses'. We all know that Death cannot talk back to us and hold a conversation, but Bunyan is correct in viewing our meditation on such a solemn subject in terms of argument or debate, objections, excuses with truth countering anything which suggests anything contrary to what must inevitably occur. For Death holds conversation with believer and unbeliever as one who does not see eye-to-eye with whom he is conversing, or as one who is a stranger instilling fear and/or fact into the heart of his hearer.

What does Death say to the sinner? He chides the sinner for believing he is secure in this life with his worldly prosperity. Death reminds him that he has come to take the sinner away from his prosperity. The sinner has not invited Death to join him for conversation but Death comes anyway, as an intruder – the sinner has no choice but to listen. Death is an unwanted guest – he breaks in and the sinner has to hear. What does Death say? Death says the sinner is frail and brittle, and cannot escape his clutches when he wishes to destroy. The sinner pathetically thinks of calling the doctor, but Death reminds him it is fruitless. Well, could Death delay his coming for a while? When Death says there can be no delay, the sinner becomes frightened because he knows he is not ready to meet God. Death says the sinner has had time to make peace with God, and he the sinner attempts to keep Death at bay by reminding Death that the termination of his life would bring on great sorrow for his family. Is there no pity? Death says he knows no pity. When he says this, the sinner suddenly sees behind Death one that looks most fearful. It is Hell, Death's friend:

'He that doth stand behind me is my friend
Hell is his name, my brother comes to see
He'll take thee to him, till thou pay thy fee.'
At last the sinner sees all is lost.

'My heart it fails, mine eyes have lost their sight,
My soul sees fire, and hellish devils too:
God fights against me also with His might,
Oh miserable, sad, and dreadful woe!'

Yet what does Death say to the saint? He answers the saint differently, for the saint does not attempt to stave off Death – rather, the saint sighs for Paradise, where Jesus is, saying, 'If I might have my choice, I would be gone'. Death seeks to alarm him by claiming the saint does not know what it is like to die, that Death will give the believer 'such a wrench' that it will take eternity to get over it. The saint replies with the comforting thought that Jesus sapped Death of his sting and even though he had slain the likes of Samson, Saul and David, the saint will 'recover' to break from Death's 'dismal band'. Death retorts he was able to kill the very Jesus in whom the saint trusts, yet the saint is quick to point out Death could not hold Jesus down. True, Death will spoil the saint's body, but the Day will come when he shall recover his body at the coming of Jesus in the clouds, when Death shall be cast at last into the flames of Hell.

It is interesting that Bunyan, when describing the discourses taking places between humans and Death, writes about saints and sinners. Remember he describes his *Profitable Meditations* as 'a Conference between Christ and the Sinner in Nine Particulars'. Since the nine particulars include the discourse between Death and the saint, Bunyan implies the saint is a sinner right to the end of time. Yes, 'the sinner is made a saint, And brought from under every curse of God', but the saint still feels 'his Father's scourging rod' (see Particular Three). Indeed, here lies the reason why Death is able to converse with the saint: the saint can be shaken by the thought of death, and can be unsettled by thought of it unless he controls his soul by good spiritual contemplation. Death talks with the saint not merely because the saint has not yet died; no, death discourses with him because he is the saint's enemy and he knows the saint can be agitated at the thought of dying. The saint is a sinful saint, capable of being afraid. Death hopes through the usually useful means of meditation to unsettle the saint.

Yet Death finds to his disappointment that 'the sinner is made a saint', and as a saint he can face Death with poise and assurance. Despite Death's barbs, accusations and rejoinders the saint is as untroubled at the end of the discourse as he was at the beginning, ready and longing to die in order to be in Paradise with Jesus. Bunyan is not suggesting that all saints will be as untroubled as the believer discoursing with Death in *Profitable Meditations* – rather, he is projecting such a believer as the complete model for all believers when facing death. The discourse between Death and a saint then serves as a deliberate contrast to the discourse between Death and the sinner. Doubtless Bunyan sought to not only make a point with any unconverted who read his *Profitable Meditations*, but sought to show as well that the saint, though troubled by doubt at some stages of his life, could face death as a saint. Thus *Profitable Meditations* became a comfort for the converted who read it.

With respect to judgment to come, Bunyan pictures Jesus speaking with comfort to the godly at His Return, and with condemnation to the wicked, who plead excuses for not believing, only to hear their objections fairly answered.

Remembering that the Ninth Particular – concerning the Day of Judgment – is said to include 'a conference between Christ and a sinner' as well, we look with interest at the scene of the Day of Judgment as Bunyan sees it in regard to the status of those before the bar. Bunyan employs the names 'the godly' and 'the wicked' to describe the two classes of men before God. In what way does the scene resemble a discourse between Christ and the sinner? Some may say Bunyan is only thinking of Christ's particular words to the wicked in terms of a discourse between Christ and the sinner. But when one studies Christ's discourse with those called the godly, it becomes apparent once again that the godly are only sinners saved by grace. Bunyan makes the point strongly that the godly deserved less than heaven. After Christ is seen calling the godly to Him by assuring them He thought about them and their place in heaven, when His enemies spat on Him at Calvary, Bunyan has Christ then saying:

> I know you have deserved none of this,
> But rather death, if you should have your due;
> But I'll forgive you all that's done amiss,
> Though I this kindness show but to a few.
>
> It was my love to give you grace in time,
> Not your deserts, and that full well you know:
> And also I did mark you to be mine,
> Even when you lived in the world below.

So Bunyan calls the saved 'godly' but makes it clear they are only distinguished from the wicked through discriminating sovereign grace. Christ has a discourse with two kinds of sinners at the judgment: one kind are saved sinners, and the other are unsaved sinners.

Now with regard to the unsaved sinners, Bunyan pictures them objecting to Christ dismissing them to hell. They claim that it was not their fault for being unbelievers. They blame bad preaching. They blame bad company. They blame overwhelming temptations. They blame the world. They blame sin. They seek Christ's forgiveness.

Christ's answer to the unsaved sinners shows their pleas are insincere: they had the chance to repent and did not. They never loathed their sin nor with sighing went to the Saviour. They were content to give way to the wickedness confronting them and surrounding them in all their circumstances. Therefore, Christ banishes them to hell while He welcomes those who are His by grace into heaven.

Finally, as part of the Ninth and last Particular drawn for us in *Profitable Meditations*, the Bedford tinker has us imagining the thoughts passing through the minds of both the godly and the wicked in heaven and hell respectively, drawing for inspiration from our Lord's account of The Rich Man and Lazarus in Luke 16. The thoughts of saint in heaven and sinner in hell alternate to highlight the vivid contrast not only between the two different eternal conditions of saint and sinner, but between the two different states of them both while on earth. For instance, the sinner bewails the fact he paid no heed to the preacher on earth when the preacher told him to 'undo' his sin, while the saint in heaven remembers how he heard of grace through the preacher and 'it broke my heart, and won me over to abhor my sin'. The sinner admits towards the end that he really cannot blame the Lord for being cast into hell:

> The fault was mine, His grace I did refuse,
> I loved sin, His name I did not fear.

With a heavy heart the sinner resigns to the truth that the more he thought of his life on earth, the more he realizes he lost it and this increases his woe. Bunyan closes *Profitable Meditations* with these words of the sinner in hell:

Let them that yet hath life and time to see
By gospel light their sin and need of grace
Take warning by these heavy sobs of me,
And see by Christ to shun this doleful place.

Towards more Profitable Meditation

What does *Profitable Meditations* teach us about meditation? Besides making clear that sound spiritual meditation may go public even if it has been a private affair in the beginning, *Profitable Meditations* shows us in two kinds of meditation the urgent need for men to give life and time to reflect on sin and salvation, as the sinner in hell bids us to do at the end of *Profitable Meditations*. One kind of meditation is one that is rather 'enforced' on us, we may say. Discourses between Satan and the tempted soul, between Christ and the sinner, between Death and the sinner, between Death and the saint are examples of this kind. This kind is intrusive, breaking in on the soul without the soul's consent. Such meditation may be somewhat fleeting and transitory by nature, but all the same it is meditation as it engages the soul, albeit unwillingly, to contemplate the things of salvation; arguing with the soul, reasoning with the soul, countering objections, advocating and championing the truth. Then on the other hand there develops the kind of meditation that is 'unforced', we may say – the kind of meditation when the heart and soul is pleased to engage in the reasoning, the arguing and reflection on the truth for its welfare.

The enforced meditation is necessary for us all – whether we are saint or sinner – since we are all blind and indifferent to the things of God without it; but it is the unforced kind that Bunyan and all true spiritual leaders seek to promote.

The forced meditation does not need promotion, but the meditation with the soul's consent does. Meditation with the soul's consent is that which the soul is loath to engage in, as it requires more laborious thinking and it consumes more time by nature. *Meditation by consent is when the saint or sinner is required to think for himself and go beyond where the enforced meditation has led him.* Perhaps this is where some confusion lies. Some Christians may think they already meditate because thoughts on the things of salvation pass through their minds during the day. Yet are those thoughts of a voluntary kind, when the soul is pleased to think on them and dwell on them and give much time to them? If the meditation is ever fleeting or transitory, one needs to ask oneself: Is this meditation altogether spiritual in the sense that my delight is in it? Is my meditation any different from that which the unbeliever experiences? All that the ungodly experiences is enforced. If we are godly, is our thinking different? Is it voluntary? More serious, more contemplative? Can we say our delight is in the law of the Lord and on His law we willingly meditate day and night?

One cannot help but feel that if more believers today thought like Bunyan, we would meditate more often than we do. Bunyan points us to the eternal issues of heaven and hell, the urgency of the soul to turn to Christ before the day of grace passes, the imminence of death, the contradiction of the Christian being content to leave himself open to doubt and temptation, the fearful consequences of spurning Christ, the staggering grace Christ gives His own. *It is no accident that with the decline in the preaching and believing of the doctrine of heaven and hell and the eternal destiny of men in these times, meditation is rarely considered in Christian circles, that is, meditation of the kind Bunyan proposed.* Christ Himself gave us a window to look at heaven and hell when He gave us an account of the Rich Man and Lazarus. Bunyan does the same. Do we quickly pass the window, or do we stop to stare and think deeply on what we see of eternity? Do we often look through that window of the hereafter and hear the praises of the godly and hear the cries of the sinners? It once grieved me to hear a leading man of a certain denomination say from the pulpit that The Rich Man and Lazarus does not teach us about the state of the furniture in heaven or the temperature of the fire of hell! No wonder that at the end of his sermon the same preacher said with exasperation, 'I do not know how to apply this parable. I leave it to you to try to do so'. Take the parable seriously and you will apply it through solemn meditation that befits such teaching from our Lord.

The Ebb and Flow of Meditation

That Bunyan also believed meditation counts for little in days of apostasy is apparent in his glorious work *The Holy War*[1].

The *Holy War* appeared in 1682 and for many Christian people over the years it has proved popular. The *Pilgrim's Progress* has been the most popular, but *The Holy War* holds a firm second place for many.

The *Holy War* sets out to recall the fall and redemption of mankind under the guise of a besieged city. This city originally belonged by right to Shaddai or God, but was betrayed through Ear Gate and Eye Gate into the hands of Diabolus or the Devil. In the hands of the enemy the city Mansoul loses its Mayor (Lord Understanding) and Mr Conscience is dismissed from his post as Recorder. Lord Will-be-Will becomes the Lord of Mansoul. However, Emmanuel sets out to recapture Mansoul, and when He does the inhabitants of the city cannot get enough of Him. Well, they cannot get enough of Him, but there are subversive forces at work inside the city. Incredulity, who had been imprisoned, escapes. He had been the Lord Mayor under Diabolus, but Understanding is given the position again when Emmanuel

---

1. A complete edition of *The Holy War*, with introduction and explanatory notes by David Porter, is published by Christian Focus Publications.

conquers the city. Incredulity, out of malice and hatred, flees the city and joins Diabolus to help him recapture it.

Diabolus discovers there are enough inhabitants of the city to help betray it, since Mansoul as a city had begun to lose its love for Emmanuel, who even withdraws from Mansoul without the inhabitants knowing! – though He leaves agents in an attempt to win back the city.

Mansoul grieves and pines for its loss. Mr Carnal Security has stripped Mansoul of its glorious towers, broken down its gates, and ruined its locks and bars. Mansoul yearns for Emmanuel to return and restore the city to its former glory and strength. It becomes a city of confusion, as friends and enemies cannot be distinguished. The Prince is taking a long time to return and win the place again.

Finally, Emmanuel returns, though the battle against Diabolus is a hard one. The return of Emmanuel guarantees that Mansoul shall never be taken captive by Diabolus again in any degree:

> The town of Mansoul did also now more thoroughly seek the destruction and ruin of all remaining Diabolonians that abode in the walls, and the dens that they had in the town of Mansoul; for there was of them that had, to this day, escaped with life and limb from the hand of their suppressors in the famous town of Mansoul.

Lord Will-be-Will becomes a greater terror than ever to the Diabolonians, many of whom are still hiding in the city after the bells have rung out when Emmanuel victoriously enters the gate. Although Lord Will-be-Will had been Lord of Mansoul before the city was taken by Diabolus, he does not become the Lord of the city again, though he is pardoned. He proves to be particularly zealous when Emmanuel has to come up to recapture the place. Lord Will-be-Will, together with Diligence, is given a commission to search out and arrest any of Diabolus' men left in Mansoul.

One particular opponent that Lord Will-be-Will seeks, arrests and executes is Mr Let-Good-Slip. We read:

> He (Lord Will-be-Will) also took Mr Let-Good-Slip one day as he was busy in the market, and executed him according to law. Now there was an honest poor man in Mansoul, and his name was Mr Meditation, one of no great account in the days of apostasy, but now of repute with the best in town. This man, therefore, they were willing to prefer. Now Mr Let-Good-Slip had a great deal of wealth heretofore in Mansoul, and at Emmanuel's coming, it was sequestered to the use of the Prince. This, therefore, was now given to Mr Meditation, to improve for the common good, and after him to his son, Mr Think-Well; this Mr Think-Well he had by Mrs Piety his wife, and she was the daughter of Mr Recorder.

Some interesting observations can be made about the return of Meditation according to the above excerpt from *The Holy War*. Bunyan reminds us that meditation loses its appeal when God's children backslide, but when they come to their spiritual senses once more and their souls are revived, then meditation becomes well accepted and regarded with considerable honour. Note that meditation has wealth to draw on when he becomes acceptable again. Christians, when they first believe, love the Lord and cannot have enough of Him. 'His person, His action, His words and behaviour were so pleasing, so taking, so desirable to them', but this knowledge of the Lord is not lost although the believer has backslidden. This is why Bunyan has us thinking in terms of Mr Let-Good-Slip. There is a wealth of knowledge not lost. The knowledge once good, still is good during the time of backsliding, and returns as good, even better, once meditation regains supremacy. It is better in the sense that it is in better hands, and it is employed more frequently in the way it was designed; the knowledge is not simply locked away in the mind as in the days of backsliding, when there is no wish to use it nor to be seen as using it.

Notice Mr Meditation distributes the wealth for the common good. What does this mean? It falls into line with the reason for Bunyan having *Profitable Meditations* published: he sought to have his thoughts on salvation made public. Bunyan was not denying that meditation is good for the believer privately, but he views meditation as that which is beneficial to the single believer and thus becomes beneficial to the Church as a consequence. How does it become beneficial to the Church? How does the wealth pass on from Mr Meditation to the rest of Mansoul? *Bunyan does not elaborate, but we can assume that he believed the nature of meditation in an individual is such that the believer spontaneously, almost unconsciously, proves to be beneficial to the Church.* Out of the abundance of his good thoughts the single believer cannot help but enrich other believers around. Bunyan rightly has the welfare of the Church in mind rather than the individual; all the same, he does not picture Mr Meditation begrudgingly distributing his wealth but doing it because it is the nature of meditation to be spontaneously generous.

Note the relatives of Mr Meditation. He has married a woman called Piety. Piety and Meditation give birth to Think-Well. Strictly speaking, meditation just for the sake of meditation is of no value, but when it is meditation on things spiritual and it is carried out with holy living in mind, then it is sound thinking. You need piety and meditation to think well. And piety is related to the conscience. Mr Recorder, father of Mrs Piety, is the conscience in *The Holy War*. Our conscience tells us to be holy before God. Everyone knows that a man is what he is according to his thoughts. We do not need a Censor Board to judge what will harm us and what will help us in our thoughts, for we all know, just as Jesus said: 'The good man brings good things out of the good stored up in his heart, and the evil man brings evil things out of the evil stored up in his heart. For out of the overflow of his heart his mouth speaks.' So meditation is related to piety and conscience and gives birth to Mr Think-Well, who has the wealth of meditation bequeathed to him, and who then distributes for the common good.

Bunyan beautifully shows us that the meditator is most conscious of his wealth of knowledge coming from the Prince Himself: 'Now Mr Let-Good-Slip had a great deal of wealth heretofore in Mansoul, and, at Emmanuel's coming, it was sequestered to the use of the Prince'.

It is not simply a matter of anyone giving Mr Meditation the wealth. It is taken away from Mr Let-Good-Slip, given to the Prince, who in turn personally gives it to Mr Meditation. Only those who meditate well will understand the beauty of Bunyan's truth at this point. One may say that the thoughts that come to the serious meditator are like the words of a love letter to the soul – they appear as the words of Jesus Himself. It is the Prince's wealth that the meditator receives; they are not simply words of ink on a page, but His precious thoughts and words of love to the craving soul. *The casual reader of the Word, the quick reader of the Word, may have an inkling of the wealth of the Word, but only those who meditate know the true value of the treasure and know how to put its currency to good use.* As they discover the inexpressible riches in deep and solemn thinking, they are conscious this is a wealth that comes from the Prince Himself, both for private well-being and the well-being that promotes the common good. And there seems no end to this wealth:

Afresh I praise Thee for Thine ever new
    And blessed Word;
  Daily it comes to me, fresh as the dew,
    This blessed Word.

Oh, be it mine, yet more and more I pray
To meditate therein both night and day!

What God hath spoken well demands our time!
  His blessed Word.
Let patient, loving toil search His sublime
  And blessed Word.
Only to meditation is it given
To taste the fulness of this truth from heaven.

Grains of this gold expand to boundless leaf;
  This blessed Word
Gives itself out to search, not survey brief,
  Oh blessed Word!
One page of thee is inexhaustible;
Nought shows eternity's employ so well.

Exhaustless is thy new, and new thine old,
  Most blessed Word;
Such wealth of folded treasure to unfold,
  Oh blessed Word,
Demands eternity! helps me to see
How endless life may endless learning be.

                          (Hymn by W. Ball)

In eternity meditation will be enjoyed with greater powers than
we now have, and anyone who now dwells much on God's Word
can appreciate how endless our learning can be. Oh, how many
believers today are content with just a passing glance at the
Scriptures, with just a trace of doctrine, with just the bare
essentials in order to be saved! Are such believers truly content
with that? Not really, they are not truly content. If only they
would draw more from the Prince's wealth than they do! Sad to
say, they often do not know why they are impoverished. If only
they could retrace their steps and recall the days when they first

believed. They could not get enough of Him then, at the time when He would speak and they would put their hands over their mouths and listen to Him, when they would copy Him as He walked around them, just as Bunyan tells us.

Those were the days Bunyan well describes as a time of great feasting, when the Prince served them what Bunyan quaintly calls 'outlandish food', that is, food they had never known before, food not of the world or the universe, but food which came from the Father's Court. Those were the days when one dish after another was set before them and they would whisper to each other, 'What is it?' for they did not know what to call it. Yes, there was wine, there was sweet music, angel's food, honey from the rock. Those were the days when Emmanuel entertained them with riddles, which were a joy to them that 'they could not have thought that such rarities could have been couched in so few and such ordinary words'. Those were the days when, as Bunyan puts it so well, 'they were transported with joy, they were drowned with wonderment. ...Yea, so taken were the townsmen now with their Prince, that they would sing of Him in their sleep'.

Arresting the decline in meditation

What has happened to you who once knew the Lord so well? Why is it the Scriptures that carried such extraordinary words for you once seem to be only rather ordinary words now? Could it be that you fell into a false security as Bunyan's Mansoul did? Has Jesus withdrawn from you? Have you noticed that you now feebly just knock once or twice on His door when you pay Him the occasional visit, and He does not seem to notice, whereas He used to run to meet you? The change is in you, not in Him. He withdrew from you gradually and you did not notice. 'And now, you boast and talk of your strength, but it is gone I tell you! Do you yearn for the return of Jesus to your soul?'

You ought not to stay backslidden. Although Jesus is not with you as you wish Him to be, you ought to be prepared to fight the enemy of your soul.

We read in *The Holy War*, however, that returning from a backslidden state may be a protracted and painful process. In Mansoul, when the townsfolk wonder at the whereabouts of the Prince, and feel the pain at His absence, they begin to take notice of a Mr Godly-Fear, who advises them to send off a petition to the Prince, 'begging Him to turn to them yet again in grace and favour and not keep His anger forever'. To their dismay the townsfolk learnt that the Prince would not see the person with the petition but told him to relay the message, 'Let them go, rather, to their friend Mr False-Security and ask him to be their lord and protector!' This makes the people mourn. Once more they seek Mr Godly-Fear's advice. He tells them that there is nothing more they can do than send another petition.

Well, one petition after another is sent. The townspeople have to learn that the wise El Shaddai (God the Father) makes men wait and exercises their patience – if they are in such great need, they should be able to wait. Mr True-Concern is one of those in Mansoul who makes moves to get rid of the enemy within.

One day out of desperation and after a long time in 'this wretched, divided condition' of Mansoul, bereft of the Prince's presence and being harassed and overrun by Diabolonians, someone suggests sending yet another petition. How can they word it? Mr Godly-Fear advises them to this effect, 'So far you have sent one petition after another and to no avail, but I now know why none of them have been successful: none of them has been signed by the Lord Secretary, nor indeed drawn up by Him'. The Lord Secretary upon their request gives them a curious answer: 'O, you must be present at the writing and you must put your desires in it. The handwriting and the pen shall be mine, but the paper and ink must be yours, else how can it be called your petition? I have no need to petition for myself for I have not offended. I will not send a petition to the Prince, and by Him to His Father, unless the people involved are in the matter heart and soul.'

The petition goes by lame Captain Faith. He goes with a sealed package. At last the Prince pays heed to Mansoul. The sealed package contains the assurance that soon the Prince will return. The town is to be left in the hands of the Lord Secretary through Captain Faith, and all will be well until the Prince returns. Even though the enemy is still strong in the town, the Lord Secretary effects a safeguarding work in preparation of the Prince's coming again, with Mr Godly-Fear being well respected for being the first man in Mansoul to detect Mr False-Security's corrupting effect on the town.

What is Bunyan saying to believers who have backslidden? Some of the things he says may appear odd to us today, but only because we are not as concerned about our souls as we ought to be, thinking that once we believe in Jesus for the first time we are completely saved and scarcely any more needs to be done.

The Church in the West today has a fixation about evangelism, so that often when people become Christians there is no longer any concern for them. We need to heed Bunyan's warning about false security. False-Security is pictured by the tinker of Bedford as lulling Mansoul into believing the town would be happy forever now that it seemed strong and safe; and Mr False-Security turns the townspeople from talking to feasting, then from feasting to sporting, relaxing into careless ways as the days pass by. Is not this a picture of the Church in this hedonistic age? Friends, no wonder Jesus is not with us as He has been with His church in the past! We need revival once more.

Turning Back to God

What does Bunyan mean when he writes about the Lord Secretary helping out with the petition that at last finds the Prince returning to Mansoul? What does he mean when he speaks of the handwriting and the pen being the Lord Secretary's, whilst the paper and the ink must belong to those of Mansoul? There is much here that the church today cannot understand and to its undoing. It is not merely that the wise El-Shaddai teaches the church to wait and to exercise patience until He is pleased to bless. It also has to do with the mind of the church before revival and restoration can occur.

In days when Mr Godly-Fear is not a favourite in the church – whoever hears from the pulpit about 'fearing God' in these times? – one needs to recall how far the church has slipped and what she must do to prepare for revival and the return of God's favour. She must begin to tremble again, she must be disturbed into repenting for her sin. While she may tremble and seek to repent, however, there is reticence on the Prince's part to return because there is still much sin within. Doubt too threatens as the church waits. Then comes the time of deep heart-searching, 'the strict and thorough search in every house from top to bottom'. Fasting and humiliation need to be sincerely observed, seeing each sin for what it really is and giving them all their proper names. For example, Mr Harmless-Fun should really be seen as Lord Loose-Living. Public confession of sin needs to be made. Then, when the Enemy makes his vicious assault in this crucial time of waiting for God to bless, the church is more than ready to face him. Still, the vicious assault is scarcely blunted, because God wants His people to feel deeply the evil of deserting Him.

The vicious assault is scarcely blunted in the sense that God's people, when they are in earnest about conquering the Enemy and are most sensitive to their own sin, often make a blind attack on the Enemy. Bunyan pictures this in terms of Mansoul calling on Captain Faith, Captain Experience and Captain Good-Hope to lead troops against the enemy at night-time.

I think we see a parallel to this in some quarters today among God's people. There are those who believe in revival, who know God is not with us as He used to be, who are troubled by their sin and by the sin in the church, but they have erred in attacking the Devil in the night. They are hitting out at the Devil blindly. They are resorting to all kinds of things to regain God's blessing, but they are doing it in their own way and by their own futile wisdom. They are sincere but they are ignorant, ignorant of the truth that until God's people cry out for help by the Holy Spirit, all previous petitioning is unprevailing.

The Lord Secretary is the Holy Spirit in The Holy War, and Bunyan is teaching us that only when the Holy Spirit is crying out for revival through us will we be heard. This crying out of the Spirit is often preceded by much heart-searching by God's people, when, like the townsfolk of Mansoul, we do everything we can to show our dislike for our enemies.

This approach in seeking God's blessing for His people may seem strange to many moderns, but, as Dr Martyn Lloyd-Jones reveals, before 1850, whenever the Christian church went into decline anywhere, God's people would resort to fervent prayer, confessing privately and publicly their sin, seeking reform until the time came for the Holy Spirit to assist their heart-rending prayers. Today we intensify our efforts for evangelism instead, set Church-growth targets and the like, without reference to sin in the church. But in yesteryear this was not the ways of God's people when they desired the prosperity of the church. Only when the Holy Spirit is petitioning, only when our heart and soul is truly in our prayers with Him will we be heard.

An incident that occurred in Wales in 1762 punctuates the

truth Bunyan expresses about the Holy Spirit. For some years revival had been experienced in Wales mainly through the powerful preaching of Daniel Rowland. But the church experienced some disquiet and decline, especially through the rift between Howell Harris, another great evangelist, and Daniel Rowland. Reconciliation was made between the two in 1762, but despite men preaching and praying as they had done before, with congregations longing and singing and sighing as they had done in the past, the church had to wait for God's time. She had to wait for the cry of the Spirit.

This came at a special prayer meeting, which some had declared would be the last, as cowardice, unbelief and the onslaughts of Satan were prevailing (see how Bunyan's imagery in *The Holy War* dovetails into this scene?). Resolved never to meet this way again, the men of the special prayer meeting were on the point of offering up a final prayer when one of the men, the most timid one and the one who felt the strongest 'in his belief that God would never visit us', began to pray in an astounding way. He began to 'lay hold powerfully on heaven as one who would not let go'. His voice grew louder. He pleaded. He cried to God. He struggled. He wrestled vehemently. The fire took hold of others and a witness later remarked: 'We all went with him in battle. With him we laid hold upon God, His attributes, His Word and His promises, resolving that we would never let go our hold until our desire should be satisfied.'

What else happened when that strong cry of the Spirit went up in what was supposed to be the last meeting? An eyewitness tells us 'the sweet breath of the love of the Lord' came upon them. Gone was unbelief, guilt, fear, cowardice, lack of love, envy, suspicion. In came love, faith, hope. Instead of closing the meeting, the men prayed on, and sang and praised God, with no one feeling that their time together should end. There was weeping, there was heavenly laughter, there was wonder and amazement at the Lord's work. All this was the beginning of another great awakening that shook the nation of Wales.

All this may seem far removed from the subject of meditation, but it helps to underline the value of meditation. *It brings home the truth that meditation, as well as being of great account in days of spiritual awakening, ought to be solemnly practised to avoid decline among God's people.* In studying *The Holy War* one can see what great devastation occurs when Mr Meditation is no longer of any repute. One can see what great price we will pay should we neglect to contemplate seriously on the things of God. In Bunyan's mind Mr Let-Good-Slip (who took Mr Meditation's place, you may remember, when the Enemy regained entry to Mansoul), was just as much a destroyer of Mansoul as Mr Fooling, Mr Slavish-Fear, Mr No-Love, Mr Mistrust, Mr Flesh and Mr Sloth. In endeavouring to cleanse Mansoul once again of its enemies, Mr Let-Good-Slip is sought after by Lord Willbewill and Diligence just as much as the other evil characters. In our day the cry to get rid of Mr Let-Good-Slip and the others aforementioned will ring hollow as we laze away our days in concession to the Enemy, but let us hope that Mr Godly-Fear is about to call us to our senses in an attempt to begin a concerted attack on the Enemy again.

We owe so much to John Bunyan for drawing attention to why meditation is of no repute in days of apostasy, and how it is of great account when the church once more knows the blessing of God.

It will be a blessed time indeed when, like a descriptive new convert of that 1762 Welsh Revival put it: 'Christ's love burns within me, ... at such time my memory is more alert, and innumerable Scriptures flood my mind. My senses are sharpened. I understand the things of God in clearer light.' There will be so much wealth then for Mr Meditation to distribute.

5

NATHANIEL MATHER

Nathaniel Mather is not read about in the annals of regular church history. Perhaps the only extant work where one can read of him is the *Magnalia Christi Americana* (The Great Works of Christ in America), a book produced by Cotton Mather, a Puritan minister who was born in Boston, Massachusetts, and who happened to be the brother of Nathaniel. Nathaniel and Cotton were sons of Increase Mather, Cotton being the eldest. Their grandfathers, Richard Mather and John Cotton, were fathers of New England and were what we know today as Pilgrim Fathers.

These Pilgrim Fathers initially came from a little village in Scrooby in Nottinghamshire, England. They lived in the time of King James I, who ordered everyone to obey the rules of the Church of England and go to its services. Anyone who refused to obey was threatened with punishment. The Puritans thought worship should be simple and based on the Scriptures, not on the Anglican Prayer Book.

They longed to worship God freely, therefore those of Scrooby made their escape to Holland, where people were allowed to live and worship as they liked. In Holland they found life difficult; they were country people who had to adapt to city life; they had to learn a new language; also, they found they could not agree with other Puritans who had also come across from England but whose worship was not all that acceptable to them. They moved to a smaller town called Leyden. There they found more content-ment, working hard to earn good money, as well as procuring a house for a meeting place. John Robinson was their pastor.

However, in their ten years at Leyden they became particularly discontent because they were afraid their children would forget they were English and forsake the simple and godly life to follow the worldly ways of the Dutch around them.

In 1620 they decided to go to America, for few people were living there at the time and they could realize their hopes of remaining English and live in an unfettered, godly way. The king, still James I, gave the Puritans permission to leave England and settle in America on condition they paid back certain merchants money lent to them, by working five days a week for seven years.

The story of the sailing of *The Mayflower* is well-known. So too the landing at New Plymouth, where they encountered many hardships and difficulties when they first settled. Yet by 1627 the Puritans had paid back their loan to the merchants.

Cotton Mather includes in his *The Great Works of Christ in America* a history of the Puritan church in the early days of settlement in America, and mainly uses individual biographies of those he regards as leading and influential figures of the time, to give us a portrait of Puritan life in the seventeenth century.

One such biography is that of his brother, Nathaniel, who is included in *The Great Works* as 'an instance of more common learning and virtue ...' Nathaniel only lived until he was nineteen years of age, but says Cotton Mather in Chapter 10 of his history of New England:

> Thou hast here a rare history of a youth, that may be of great use and advantage both to old and young; that the aged, seeing themselves outdone by green years, may 'gird up their loins', and mend their pace for heaven; and that young ones may be so wrought into the love of religion, as it is exemplified in this holy person, as to endeavour with all diligence to write after his excellent copy.

Matthew Mead, who prefaces the biography of Nathaniel Mather with an introductory note, writes beautifully that God does not gather the fruit of any man's life until it is ripe. Some of us live long only because the fruit takes a long time to develop. We are not in the world simply to live out a certain number of years, but to fill up our measure of grace. Whenever that is done, God takes us from this earth. When Nathaniel Mather died at nineteen, the fruit had already ripened – he had come to his grace not untimely but 'at full age like as a shock of corn comes in his season'.

Nathaniel's brother, Cotton, before he begins his biography of his brother, says by way of introduction that they who 'live in heaven while they are on earth' often 'live on earth after they are in heaven'. He attempts to be modest in his appraisal of his brother, claiming he is out to evoke followers and not admirers of his brother. Cotton says his brother lives on, speaking through his death. He was his brother close at hand and believes Nathaniel can be a brother by faith to any reader.

The life of Nathaniel Mather is unique to the study of Puritan meditation. Here we gain insights in a more practical way of what meditation meant to the Puritans. Mather inherited the godly, Puritan and spiritual tradition of 'chewing the cud'. It was a rich tradition, with men such as Thomas Watson, William Bridge, John Owen, George Swinnock, Thomas Manton, William Gurnall, Stephen Charnock and Richard Baxter showing the way.

He knew that meditation was rated as the best beginning for prayer and its best conclusion. He knew that to meditate is to fill your vessel so full of good thoughts that there is no room for evil ones. He knew meditation worked on a man's feelings and emotions and warmed them as wind blows on a fire. He knew meditation was the measuring stick by which one measures his spirituality. He knew meditation is the best way to combat solitariness, when the enemy has a good chance to stir up sinful desires. He doubtlessly was taught there is much to meditate on – in fact, no end to subject matter. He knew it to be a hard work but knew that love for his Lord made it easier. He knew sermons were to be thought about, and meditation causes any worthwhile sermons to be remembered. He knew meditation is the means by which we fall in love – fall in love with our Maker. Yes, he knew 'in secret thought chewing the cud of every circumstance with continual contemplation'.

He was born on July 6th, 1669 and quickly became a good scholar as a child, when it is said a book was as dear to him as play. Nathaniel was such an avid student of books that his candle would burn after midnight in his pursuit of learning. It appears he studied too much as a youngster, so that by the age of sixteen his neglect of moderate physical exercise caught up with him, leaving him with pains that hastened him onto death three years later. At the tender age of twelve he had been admitted to college by 'strict examiners'.

Not many months after being admitted, he had accurately gone over all the Old Testament in Hebrew and the New Testament in Greek, besides studying the liberal sciences. He commenced his B.A. at sixteen and 'in the act entertained the auditory with a Hebrew oration which gave a good account of the academical affairs among the ancient Jews'. He knew Hebrew so well that if circumstances had called for it, he could have used Hebrew as the only language for communication. Although he was a person of few words, his knowledge on all kinds of subjects was remarkable.

From when he was very young, the gospel in its purity had made some impression on him to the extent he would spend time in secret prayer for his soul. It seems, however, that at the age of twelve he began in earnest to thirst for Christ and to remain no more apathetic about the things of salvation. Until the age of fourteen he was 'following hard after God', thinking of death and its consequences if he should neglect the command of Christ to obey the gospel.

His conversion certainly did not come about in a rash, brief moment. As he was 'following hard after God', he took careful note of the vileness of his sins; noticing that pride, unthankfulness and the failure to make good use of the means of grace were to be lamented. Realizing what graces he needed to be saved, and what mercies already had been his as a means for learning about the gospel, Nathaniel resolved to dedicate himself to God.

After thinking much, reading much, writing much and praying much, he entered into a covenant with God. This covenant he put down in writing for several reasons: firstly, by writing it down he believed it would make more impression on his heart and life; secondly, it would be a sober record to be reminded about when temptation or distress arose.

The written covenant did not prevent him from experiencing an unhappy and gradual apostasy. For many months he was divested of that wisdom and virtue that had been such a sound testimony of the grace within him before. In the year 1685, 'God visited him with sore terrors and horrors in his wounded soul, the anguish whereof he thought intolerable...' and it is believed that until his dying day he walked constantly and faithfully with his God: 'For more than the last three years of his life, he lived at a strange rate for holiness and gravity...'

Two books had a profound influence on him, one of which was John Owen's *Spiritual Mindedness*. John Owen, the great Puritan who served Oliver Cromwell as chaplain, makes it clear one cannot have life and peace in the soul unless one detaches himself from the world in his mind, and sets himself apart to becoming spiritually-minded. The world comes to us in many voices, comes to us with countless hard-sell approaches, and comes to us with urgency. We can only withstand such pressure by not leaving room or time for the world's entertainment.

The young Mather was amazed at the absence of spiritual-mindedness among many believers, who seek to gain life and peace without it. Owen argues that just as the men of the world, whose minds are carnal, are constantly excited by their corrupt affections, thoughts, meditations and desires, so those who are spiritually-minded ought to be continually influenced by thoughts and meditations of spiritual things, and with delight and satisfaction. Although Mather wondered if he could ever reach such a high degree of spiritual-mindedness as that set out by Owen, he strove for the rest of his life to live a life wholly spent for God, strictly and secretly. Says his brother, Cotton: 'He withdrew from the delights of this world, and gave himself up to an assiduous contemplation of God and Christ, and a sedulous endeavour after utmost conformity unto Him'.

Nathaniel Mather was determined not to be the kind of unspiritual man described by John Owen in an early part of his *Spiritual Mindedness*. Owen claims true spiritual-mindedness does not rise and fall according to renewed convictions that occur from time to time. Some fall into thoughts full of God whenever God rebukes them, when fear of death looms, and so on, but such thoughts soon fade away. True spiritual-mindedness is only evident when the 'spirited thoughts' are even and constant, 'unless an interruption be put upon them for a season by temptations'. It is rather like measuring the fertility of soil. Where one both tills and manures the soil and it brings forth a good harvest, one knows the soil is excellent, the manure merely using the potential of the good soil to produce a healthy crop. If one tills land and manures the soil, and then finds the harvest only appearing where the manure was laid, it can be concluded the soil is barren, since of itself it cannot produce anything.

God provides means of grace for many, for the stirring up of holy thoughts and feelings, but in some they only occasionally serve their purpose since they 'spring only from the notions of things prospered unto them', while in others 'they excite the inward principle of the mind to act in holy thoughts, according unto its own sanctified disposition and prevalent affections'. Mather was determined to prove to himself he could be constantly spiritual because he possessed the sanctified disposition required.

Firstly, he 'walked by rule'. He resolved to regulate his life by the Word of God. He had in mind his thoughts, his feelings, his delights. Through the Word he set his mind on what should be his fear, what should be his hope, what should be his hatred, what should be his trust. His speech and work were to be regulated by the Word as well. A hymn of his own composition reinforced such resolve. Then, the young man took to living by God's promises as well as God's precepts. To make use of such promises he set them out like this in order to recall them daily. 'Let me salute these promises once a day':

1. For supplying the wants of the day, Philippians 4:19.
2. For growth in grace, Hosea 14:5.
3. For subduing my sins, Micah 7:9.
4. For success in my undertakings, Psalm 1:3.
5. For turning all of the events of the day for good, Romans 8:28.
6. For audience of my prayers, John 14:13,14.
7. For strength to manage all the work of the day, Zechariah 10:12.
8. For direction in difficulty, Psalm 3:8.
9. For life eternal, Luke 12:31, Job 3:16.

Besides these two, Matthew 11:28 and Isaiah 44:3.

Secondly, Nathaniel Mather lived by prayer. It would appear that unless circumstances prevented it, he would go to prayer at least three times a day, wrestling 'in them for a good part of an hour together'. The young man puts on record that at times he even prayed in his sleep, on occasions when the devil sought to take advantage of him and planted in his mind various temptations, which he countered with quick prayers that made 'the phantasms to leave annoying him'.

He shared John Owen's belief that a believer prays not only because it is a duty, but because he knows he stands in need of it. Indeed he cannot live without it, 'and to keep them from it, is all one as to keep them from their daily food and refreshment'. There were days when the young man went without food and fasted as he prayed. On such days it was his custom to make a detailed confession of all the sins of which he knew he was guilty.

He renewed his covenant with the Holy One of Israel. To determine what exactly were his sins, he had written an extensive catalogue of all the 'things forbidden and required in the commands of God', this catalogue being the objective mirror by which to judge himself.

In case a modern should think that such founding fathers of America spent their time only in the morbidity of confessing their sins, remember many in those times also spent days purely reserved for thanksgiving as well. In this Mather and others of his time followed the godly ways of many of the Puritans whom they left behind in England, Puritans such as Thomas Watson, who said: 'Praising God is one of the highest and purest acts of religion. In prayer we act like men; in praise we act like angels.' Nathaniel called days set aside for thanksgiving 'a sublimer way of drawing near to God', thus indicating that the Puritans not only sensed the danger of occupying one's mind too much in examining oneself for the confession of sin to the point of being despondent and circling around in gloom, but knew the praising of God to be of nobler exercise in adoring Him who is greater than man and who deserves all the praise we can render.

Mather, knowing that others had gone before him in this very fruitful exercise, was not willing to leave such a thing unattempted. Consequently, he resolved every two months to set aside one day for 'solemn examination and meditation' and one day for 'private thanksgiving'. All this, that is, his constant and daily private prayer and days spent in examination and thanksgiving, as well as time spent in corporate prayer and thanksgiving with neighbouring believers.

Thirdly, he thought much about God. Stephen Charnock, the Puritan whose fame chiefly lies in his great work *Existence and Attributes of God*, had preached a sermon in England about Thoughts, and young Mather wrote out for himself a copy of that sermon, 'chewed much' on it and 'made it the very mould of his gracious mind'.

Regarding his method for meditation on things directly spiritual we read in *Magnalia Christi Americana* it was the teenager's habit to reflect on some truth or some text for a good part of an hour each morning. This he did, basing his meditation on a good variety of subjects and Scripture for that purpose. At times when he was meditating in this way, he would also write down the fruit of his thoughts, not always all that he thought but in brief what had passed through his mind.

We have on record some of the things he meditated on: 'The reason I have to love God, the nature of the soul and the body, the body as the soul's instrument'. This was Mather's way for what we may call 'set meditation', that is, meditation undertaken when work and the duties of this world do not interfere. Yet his cogitation was not limited to that good part of an hour in the morning.

In the course of the day, as he went about his activities, Mather would meditate on God according to the mundane things of life.

For instance, when he had to arise on a cold morning from bed, he thought of the extreme cold but resolved to dress quickly and become warm in the clothes he was to wear for the day. This act of rising in the cold was applied to spiritual truth:

> There is a necessity of rising out of my bed, the bed of security which I am under the power of, and to live unto Christ, and to walk in the light. In order hereunto, I must put on my poor soul the garments which are to be had from the Lord Jesus. To awake me out of my sleep and security, I am to set before the sun (of the gospel of righteousness) ... I am also taught that when men are convinced of their miserable condition, they will rather endeavour to please and comfort and cherish themselves by something in themselves than put on the spiritual garments which the Lord Jesus Christ has provided for them. An evil to be by me avoided.

Cotton, in showing us the way his brother meditated, calls this method 'a more delightful and surprising *(sic)* way of thinking'. Some may find this strange coming from a Puritan, who regarded very highly the meditation of Scripture, the Word of God.

Is he claiming the meditation on that derived from the mundane to be superior to the meditation of the Word? That could not be, since the Puritans believed the Word of God to be the most supreme form of revelation, the only safe guide for a holy life and right thinking. One Puritan, doubtless representing Puritan thinking as a whole, likened Scripture to the sun and the church to a clock. We take notice of clocks and they are fine if they are keeping the time; but when they are out of time, we check the time by the sun.

The Puritans did not set creation above the Word either. Still, they believed the whole creation was full of God, 'and that there was not a leaf of grass in the field, which might not make an observer to be sensible of the Lord' (Cotton Mather). To the believer the Scriptures are paramount, and in their light creation then reveals much.

The fact that Nathaniel Mather applied spiritual truth, truth that can only come from the Word, to the mundane situation of getting out of bed, proves Scripture had precedence over any other source for right thoughts. Well, why was this form of meditation described as more delightful in particular? Simply because meditation was viewed as that which is necessary for the whole course of our day, yes, even in the midst of the mundane.

Because the whole creation is full of God, it does not matter where we are or what we are doing, we should always be able to apply spiritual truth. While holding that set, deliberate and prolonged meditation in solitude is essential, it is argued by Cotton Mather that we would lose much time in thinking of God if we restricted ourselves purely to only the set, deliberate and prolonged occasions. One hour or so was spent by Nathaniel Mather in the morning – yet what of all the rest of the waking time of day? Since life is short, we are wasting time if we allow all those hours to pass by without thinking somehow on our God. As we go about doing the mundane, naturally we must give our best for what we are doing so as to bring glory to God, but all the same 'between our more stated business' there are those 'little fragments of hours', as Cotton Mather quaintly calls them, when we can meditate. This is when – to use Cotton Mather's turn of phrase – we can find filings of gold and silver to be precious.

Meditation in those 'little fragments of hours' can be spent directly thinking of Scripture too, but in *Magnalia Christi* the reference is to the meditation which springs up from things seen around us. It is both a delightful and 'surprising' way to meditate, for not only is creation full of God, but there is joy in discovering how Scripture can be applied to the mundane and it is surprising how often the mundane can be ready for the application of the Word.

Another interesting illustration and application of Scriptural truth, as recorded by Cotton Mather and according to his brother's diary, is a further example of what can be achieved by adopting this form of meditation, brief though such a form of meditation may be. Nathaniel was once sitting with some men in a room that was only lit by one candle. One of the men began to read. Then another candle was brought in. This made the reading easier. Here is the application:

> 'That those who are to be the teachers of others have need of as much light again as ordinary Christians have. They, if any, need a double portion of the gifts that are in other men; and the helps of knowledge that other people have, they much more should be furnished withal. It was not because they had better eyes than him whose office it was to read, that they needeth but one candle, when he had two provided for him; but the work incumbent on him and expected from him was the occasion for it.'

One can see that meditation of this kind requires a certain skill and a knowledge of God's Word. Firstly, a knowledge of God's Word is acquired; and then the skill to apply it in the common and what seem trivial occasions of life to make such times moments for thinking great thoughts about God. By the way, this skill of making meditation spring from things seen around us is the reason why the Puritans were such attractive preachers. It is true that a good many of them could well be criticized for labouring a point or two, but one cannot help but admire the genius in what are known in our times as 'illustrations' in sermons. The word 'genius' is used aptly. It can be argued that anyone can take an illustration or two and use it in a sermon. The Puritans were different: one feels their many 'illustrations' were different in the sense that they were not contrived, but they were original to them as preachers and were the fruit of their constant meditation and close observation of God's creation.

Charles Spurgeon, the famous Baptist preacher of the last century, once published a book which was subtitled *Flowers From a Puritan Garden,* a collection of Thomas Manton's illustrations and similes. Said Manton, 'The end of study is information, the end of meditation is practice, or a work upon the affections. Study is like a winter's sun that shineth but warmeth not; but meditation is like blowing up the fire, where we do not mind the blaze but the heat.' The likes of Manton did not depend on the paint of words, for they knew that only bred 'painted grace' – no, to change the metaphor, they possessed the fruit that had been exposed to plenty of sun, and the sunlight of God's Word conjoined with their persistence in applying it to things around them. The Puritans preached with great power and conviction, with the Spirit, and with the arresting ability to bring home the truth through frequent application to common things.

Nathaniel Mather was no preacher, but he felt the need as a layman to employ this kind of meditation for his own spiritual advantage.

After telling us that his brother meditated according to 'a more delightful and surprising way of thinking', Cotton tells us, as we may expect, that it was the 'Book of God' that was Nathaniel's principal source for thinking. He tells us quaintly that he (Nathaniel) 'was very expensive on his thoughts on the "Book of God".' Even when the young man was nearing death and quite ill, he was angry with himself if he did not have read to him a part of the Bible each day. He took to reading notes which had been composed by certain preachers of the Word not long before he died, but the dying man felt there was nothing compared with the actual reading of Scripture, together with making his own notes and drawing out of the Word an observation and a prayer out of every verse he read.

At evening he gave himself up to much spiritual thinking too. This not only led to sleeping peacefully, but made it possible to get a better understanding of himself through 'three general questions' he put to himself:

Question 1: What has God's mercy been to me this day?
Question 2: What has my carriage to God been this day?'
Question 3: If I dye *(sic)* this night, is my immortal spirit safe?

Even a moral heathen has told us that wisdom consists in examining ourselves each night, Mather noted, and he concluded that a Christian, who is more clear-headed than an unbeliever, ought more certainly to have the practice. The three questions gave rise to seeing whether or not he had as his greatest motive in life the glory of God. These three questions were also looked at side-by-side with the marks and signs of one born of God, as the Scripture has them.

A modern believer may wonder why a child of God need ask the aforementioned third question, 'If I die tonight, is my immortal spirit safe?' But in the eyes of the Puritans a child of God always needed to examine himself for the purpose of being assured he is a child of God, particularly when death nears and threatens to have us doubt our salvation. Someone may ask, 'Did Nathaniel Mather have assurance from days before – why seek it each day?' The earnest believer knows each day brings its own troubles, each day requires a renewed effort to gain certainty of hope, particularly if the days are drawing nearer to death. So, the young man did not go to asleep until he kept his soul awake.

Fourthly, Nathaniel Mather mortified and conquered the sins that were a vexation to him. One should never think that because a believer walks strictly by the rule of God, lives by prayer and thinks much about God, that he will see no trouble. Indeed, such a child of the Lord will keenly feel the barbs of Satan. Mather was no exception. In his case there were some sins which gave him 'a more violent and outrageous *(sic)* disturbance that he could without much passion bear', but the most vexatious temptation for him was blasphemy. This temptation, says Cotton Mather, may come because of our sincerity, because of our deep respect for God. When actually dying, Cotton's brother complained, *'Horrenda de Deo* (horrible conceptions of God) are buzzing around in my mind'. Once he had written in his diary:

> Troubled exceedingly with blasphemous suggestions, my soul bleeds at the thought of them. O that Christ would deliver me from them! They make my life unpleasant. I do believe that Satan never struggled so hard to keep anyone from Christ, as he has done me!

He went to the Word to strengthen himself against such assaults, wanting to know Christ as a complete Redeemer, that God's power is infinite and that God would perfect holiness where He began it in Nathaniel's soul.

Fifthly and lastly, he seemed to be acutely aware of the changes that were before him. To prepare for the pain he fortified his soul through communion with God and examination of the strength he needed to face it. According to his diary he once lamented that he had not given enough time for serious meditation in the morning. This led to deadness of spirit for the day. But more than that: it led to the fear that such a deadness of spirit ought not to be his, for how could he undergo the great trials and conflicts that were coming? He resolved to acquire a great measure of grace, to meditate more seriously. He resolved to be renewed every day. How would he achieve the great measure of grace? By earnest prayer, by holy walking, by having great feeling by the truth, by looking to Jesus, by thinking solemnly, by much reading and by expressing thankfulness to God for the knowledge he already had.

The description of the nineteen-year-old's death lends credence to the realism of the whole account of his life as told by his brother. Cotton declares that Nathaniel did not die overly happy or assured. The young man was dying of a tumour. He experienced no rapture or thrills of joy. He was afraid, afraid of being a hypocrite. He was not despairing, but he was dejected. He knew grace, but he was not joyful. While in better days health-wise he had been convinced he 'followed hard after God', and while in life he was saying such things as, 'I had fear lest I should not love the blessed God; but yet I was sure I desired to keep His commandments', while dying he was loath 'to own a clear title to God'. Still, he died with some hope in his heart. All this points to the account of Nathaniel's life being a truthful account; it would have been easy for his brother to exaggerate a little and give the account a happy ending. It must be no filial exaggeration when we read of Nathaniel's life as described by his brother as 'an instance of unusual industry and no common piety'.

That he was of unusual industriousness and unusual spirituality is testified by an 'R.H.', who composed some lines as an epitaph for Nathaniel. He wrote in effect that Nathaniel lived in heaven while he was on the earth, that he was more like a ninety-year-old in his learning than a nineteen-year-old, that he was young in years but showed full growth in grace.

We may think that it would be impossible to meditate to that length without becoming mentally unbalanced. Can one meditate for an hour each morning, meditate in snatches all day as long as he applies spiritual truth to what he sees around him, and then meditate in the evening in a set way before going to sleep? We must remember that the Puritans did not fail to see the problem, and the wise words of Richard Baxter were no doubt heeded in the days of the Puritans:

> Do not overdo in violence or length; but carry on the work sincerely according to the abilities of your minds and bodies; lest going beyond your strength you craze your brains, and discompose your minds, and disable yourselves, to do anything at all. Though we cannot estimatively love God too much, yet it is possible to think of Him with too much passion, or too long at once, because it may be more than the spirit and the brains can bare... You little know how lamentable and distressed a case you will be in, or how great an advantage the tempter hath, if once he do but tire you by overdoing.

These words of Baxter are both wise and weighty, and pay reading more than once. Still, such advice is a caution only for a few. Few over-reach when it comes to meditation, and many there will be who will take Baxter's advice in isolation. Some will say, 'I have had a struggle with meditation' and fear that which Baxter warns us about will come upon them, when their struggle actually has to do with not meditating enough, rather than meditating too much.

Baxter, you may recall, says there will be a struggle in this for all who wish to do it, and it has to do with our sinful nature opposing it. He tells us to struggle on, even if the world (and this will include the worldly believer) thinks we are doing too much, when we solemnly use the powers of our soul to think so frequently and so solidly. The over-reaching is not to be measured by what the world thinks but what our conscience, as well as our finite body and soul, tells us. This advice, you must remember, comes from one who spent at least an hour each day in thinking on eternity, and doubtlessly meditated in the same way as Nathaniel Mather did during the day, by reflecting on things around him in everyday life. Perhaps there were times when Baxter himself over-reached and this is why he could write so feelingly on this subject.

How do we know when we have over-meditated? With very few exceptions most people will know. Just as we know we have over-reached when preparing for exams and we need to take some kind of break to relax the mind, so with regard to meditation. According to our ability and the constitution of our body we can meditate until we feel in our mind that we are unsettled with too much mental gymnastics. It is time then to listen to some music or do something essentially physical.

We must remember the worth of meditation is not to be measured by the length of time spent on it, but by the impression such meditation makes. Once it has done its work of stirring the soul, then no more stirring need be done. There are no casuistic rules to follow. Once we have reached the state of delight in those things we are thinking on, there will be no weariness, so says John Owen. We may add that any weariness that arises is not weariness of the subject, but a weariness of the mind and/or the body. Such weariness ought not to be equated with spiritual weariness.

6

JOHN CALVIN

John Calvin (1509–1564) was a great French Reformer, and with Martin Luther became the two leading figures of the Reformation in Europe during the sixteenth century, shaking the foundations of a faithless, humanistic Church with the authority of the original gospel. Only forty years after Luther first protested against certain evil practices of the Roman Catholic Church, Protestantism was established in nearly half of Europe, and Calvin played no small part in this great movement of the Holy Spirit. The Reformation undoubtedly was the greatest revival the church has ever known since the days of the apostles.

Calvin was born at Noyon in France, the son of Roman Catholics. His parents wanted him to become an eminent figure in the church. He was an exceptional student, and at the age of twenty-two, in Paris as a humanist scholar, he often lectured to his fellow students in the absence of the teachers. Calvin possessed a remarkable memory and doubtless it was developed through an early habit he acquired in Paris as a student, when from day to day he used to go over all that he had learned for the day just before he went to sleep. All his life he was dogged by illness – it has been calculated that by the age of 50 he had something like forty different ailments and diseases – but he always had an amazing memory.

At twenty-three he experienced conversion. The story of how he was pressed into joining William Farel in reforming Geneva in Switzerland is well-known. An unknown person recognized the frail introvert as he sought to pass through the Swiss town on his way to Strassburg and went and told the red-headed, fiery Farel: 'John Calvin, the author of *The Institutes of the Christian Religion,* is here.'

The Institutes of the Christian Religion is still seen today as Calvin's major contribution to theology. He wrote it when he was about twenty-five years of age. The astounding thing is that while it was published in Basle in 1536, and even though Calvin added to it and republished it all through his life, the basic theology undergirding the work never changed. Of *The Institutes* Martyn Lloyd-Jones has written:

> This is undoubtedly his masterpiece. Indeed one could say that no book has had such an influence on man and on the history of civilization. It is not too much to say either that it was the *Institutes* which saved the Protestant Reformation for this was the *summa theologica* of Protestantism and the clearest which the evangelical faith has ever had.

To many young people in the Western world today, this appraisal of the *Institutes* may seem an exaggeration at a time when the foundations are being shaken, but the foundations of modern society have rested on the *Institutes* far more than many realize today. As Martyn Lloyd-Jones goes on to reveal: It was the *Institutes* that shaped the development of the Protestant churches which would arise out of the sixteenth century.

The diffident Reformer was to spend the rest of his days in Geneva after Farel compelled him to share in the ministry there, that is, except for about two years after he and Farel were banished from Geneva.

Calvin exerted an amazing influence on the life of Geneva in his time, more by personal than by political influence (Calvin did not have the right to vote in Geneva until he was 50). His influence was essentially exercised by the preaching of God's Word. At first he preached twice on Sunday, once on Monday,

Wednesday and Friday until 1542 when, after he was asked to preach more frequently, he preached every weekday on alternate weeks, and twice on a Sunday – that is, ten times a fortnight.

Calvin's influence went beyond Geneva. Not only did Geneva become the haven of 6,000 refugees which swelled the population to 20,000, but France, which only had one Reformed church in 1555, in six years saw 2,150 churches arise largely through the efforts of the indefatigable Reformer. Moreover, many of those who sought refuge in the Swiss city finally returned to their homelands to model their churches on the Genevan pattern.

As well as preaching prolifically, Calvin wrote 4,271 sermons! Many of the letters were to churches. He could rightly say, 'My sons are to be found all over the world'.

Although he was buried in a simple coffin in an unmarked grave at 54, Calvin will always be remembered as a champion of God's truth through his preaching, his counsel and his theology. Although learned, his attitude was biblical, without speculation and with fidelity to the text in his exposition of the Word. He was not verbose, he was not overly-imaginative, but he preached with great power and conviction and remarkable insight. Someone has said that to read the history of Western civilization without reference to Calvin is 'to read history with one eye shut'.

Considering Calvin from the viewpoint of meditation, we shall look at certain sermons he preached on 2 Samuel as representative of what he always preached by way of exposition, and then letters he wrote in which he makes references to the need for careful thinking.

Firstly, Calvin shows in sermons he preached on 2 Samuel[1] just what a preacher is able to do with penetrative application of

---

1. *Sermons on 2 Samuel*, translated by Douglas Kelly, published by Banner of Truth Trust, Edinburgh.

the text. Probably since the days of the apostles no one has excelled like Calvin did in this regard.

To view 2 Samuel through the eyes of Calvin one finds strikingly that he is more than a spectator of the likes of David, Jacob, Saul and Abner; he finds himself in the likes of David, Jacob, Saul and Abner.

Calvin successfully bridges the gap that some may think exists between us and those who 3,000 years ago passed through the events of 2 Samuel, as he shows that time makes no distinction when it comes to human frailty, fears and sin. We constantly see ourselves in the Word in the way those ancients acted and re-acted, as Calvin relentlessly and rivetingly applies, applies, applies. This is what makes his sermons so timeless, so invaluable. As Douglas Kelly, a translator of Calvin's 2 Samuel sermons, has said, 'We are not long in the presence of Saul and Abner, Samuel and Jonathan, David and Bathsheba, Nathan and Solomon before we are introduced to Another.' Yes, He is chiefly the one with whom we have to do. In this way Calvin is both a great preacher and pastor.

This French Reformer shows us in the second sermon on 2 Samuel that God has given us the Scriptures, which ought to be read with energy. In reference to a book we have now lost – called 'the Book of the Law' – Calvin says God caused it to be lost because He knew that in our laziness we could hardly cope with the instruction that is extant. Calvin insists the books that do remain are sufficient for our salvation, and ought to be mastered since 'the matters are not drawn out in length, with the result that we do not have to occupy ourselves a great deal with them'. We think we have done enough if we have read only one tenth of the Word! How cold and listless we are in the study of the doctrine of God!

The Pursuit of God's Will
This Word of God is sufficient for our guidance and the discernment of the Lord's will. In reference to David asking God if he ought to go up to one of the towns of Judah, when it was a terrible trial for David to be outside of Israel because he was among enemies in the Philistines at Ziklag, John Calvin emphasizes that men of the world may exercise a certain degree of prudence whenever they plan to do something, but true prudence always lies in why we are doing what we are doing. The Christian's wisdom lies in ascertaining God's will.

How do we discern His will? Firstly, 'we must come to the Holy Scripture, where God tells us what is to be done'. Secondly, all the doctrine and insight of the Holy Scripture must be blessed to us by the Holy Spirit. Yes, 'even when we have been clearly taught by His Word what is good and right, we still need God to give us an understanding of His will that, being enlightened by His Spirit, we will understand what He has said to us in His Word'. Yet this is not all, says the Reformer: we may still be undecided about several things, in which case 'we must call on the Lord, and turn to Him'. Calvin is afraid lest we become self-assured so that even after studying God's Word, we fail to pray that God will show us what is useful and expedient. Calvin spends much time on this point, drawing out all the nectar he can possibly obtain from the flowering truth that David sought God for counsel.

Submitting to God's Will
Again, Calvin chides us for our slackness, this time in regard to not submitting to God's authority. He does this when he writes on Ishboseth being killed by traitors, when Mephiboseth is crippled after his legs are broken. Says the Reformer: 'This tale will seem nothing to us but tiresome history. We could read a

hundred times that Ishboseth was killed by traitors and that Mephiboseth was crippled ...'. He goes on to tell us what the intention of God is in recording such incidents, saying that such things are never understood by natural reason. In this instance God shows that He must overcome the children of Israel in such a way that they have no choice but to submit to David.

And God must overcome us who are 'slack, slow and cold as ice' so that all opportunities for us to be prevented from submitting to the greater David are gone. One feels that while this may be a word for unbelievers to submit, we as Christians are to pay heed as well in knowing 'there is such a perversity in men that they will never be disposed to obey God and our Lord Jesus Christ (freely), if He does not force them to do so...'

When all the tribes finally submit to David, we see men, who formerly were adverse to David ruling and who were content to be under the dynasty of Saul, coming to their senses by putting aside their evil passions which caused them to misjudge and err badly. If 'we want to judge properly, we must strip ourselves of all our passions. Even when it involves some definite fact, let us continue to hold ourselves suspect, until we have learnt deliberately to despise all that can affect either our own gain or loss, or which can turn us away from judging as we should'.

Calvin says we must *carefully* observe this when it comes to the doctrine of salvation. *When we are 'besieged' by God's Word, we ought not then to be blinded and guided by our own passions.*

When the Reformer moves on to consider David going up to attack the Jebusites, whom God had condemned so long ago but who remained in the land because 'laziness kept the people (of Israel) from acting virtuously to win the country which God had given them for a heritage', he shows us the people of Israel had been stupid. Certainly, God had not yet declared that He intended to build a temple there, but the stronghold of the Jebusites was a notable location – besides, it had been ennobled because Melchizedec had his throne there in the days of Abraham.

Calvin maintains the people of God should have done 'some good reasoning within themselves', that they 'should have examined themselves in this way'. They should have meditated by looking at themselves, noticing they lacked what God promised by looking at their sins. The Reformer claims that such a lack of meditation leads to many disputes in the Christian church. Instead of looking at ourselves when it is obvious that the church has come far short of what God has promised, we engage in wrangling and breaking up the one brotherhood among us. Unity of faith could be attained if we saw that the church is not plagued and corrupted by enemies because God has frustrated our hope – no, we ourselves in the church are the enemies of God when the church is in despair. The people of God ought not to be in despair. We ought to be confident, believing He can give us what He has promised. Therefore, we ought to consider how far removed we are from the promises of God – examine ourselves and ask pardon for our faults.

If what Calvin says is true, what trouble we inherit, all because we neglect the simple exercise of taking time to reason and examine ourselves! We are like the old lady who swallowed the fly, who in turn swallowed a spider to catch the fly, and so on. Christians argue and dispute, wrong reasons fly about for their congregations' demise, and all mounting kinds of remedies are suggested for their congregations' revival until 'pure religion is torn in pieces'.

Coping with Revival

Yet when pure religion is on the rise and God is favouring us again, we still must keep our sense of reason. Calvin is fond of using such expressions as 'let us note carefully' and 'let us consider carefully'. In regard to God letting us enjoy friendly relations with unbelievers, these kind of expressions are employed without exception, when there may be less inclination to meditate and think as carefully as we should.

Calvin does not say this explicitly, but the church always faces the dangers of despair and flattery – the former arises from persecution and the latter arises from the favour of men.

When persecution fails to bring believers to despair, then comes the favour of men in the form of flattery to bring about our downfall. Therefore, whether we are being persecuted or flattered, we always need to think carefully. When God allows us to enjoy friendly relationships with unbelievers – and this may well arise because we have earned their respect by weathering persecution well – we should be careful not to make an alliance with such.

What does Calvin himself say? He could have well considered David commanding Hiram's respect, but his own emphasis is on King Hiram sending David presents and David in return agreeing to make an alliance. Calvin says David erred at this point. He says David should have been content to accept the gifts and be friends with Hiram, but not to form an alliance with the man whereby prejudice was formed against God and His church. He says Hiram gave gifts to David not because he was liberal in himself, but because God moved him to do so. David should have seen that the giving of the gifts was a sign from God that God was with him and wanted to bless his reign – instead, David attributed falsely the gifts to Hiram's generosity. This was against the honour that ought to have been attributed to God. Moreover, such an alliance as David made leads to the believer making too many concessions. He says 'we should most carefully consider this point', as 'often God is betrayed when one concedes many things which are against His honour and do harm to His cause'.

(By the way, attributing Hiram's giving to being moved by God and not by Hiram's own generosity is consistent with the doctrine Calvin sets forth in his *Institutes* to account for the reason why men, who are totally depraved by sin in body, mind and heart, are able to do seemingly good things.)

Proneness to Falling

Now, the failure to meditate on the things of God may not be sudden. It may be a slow process. Calvin claims this was true of David, and what actually led David to commit the sin of adultery.

David had for some time been polygamous. In his polygamy he had failed to watch himself carefully, says Calvin. David had flattered himself over a period of time by having more than one wife. 'But the more he flattered himself, the more God permitted him to be, as it were, alienated from his own sense, and *his memory to be totally buried.* He would have remained like a stupid and incorrigible man if God had not put His hand on him.'

David abused the institution of marriage. He had never ravished anyone else's wife previously, but in going through 'the superficial formalities of marriage' with a number of women, David had 'corrupted the order of God', and made a villainous and profane confusion of it. It caused him to become permanently blind, and in the end he became a traitor and murderer in order to commit adultery, which was an even greater evil.

Sin badly affects our memory. We see this not only with respect to David committing adultery, but in David failing to bring the Ark of God in the correct manner to Jerusalem. Although the Law of God expressly stated how the Ark was to be always transported, David, together with the high priest and the Levites, did not know what was expressly stated. How sin corrupts the memory! 'What was the cause of this failure except that the people had increasingly adulterated themselves, were not accustomed to the worship of God, and were ignorant of the simple elements of it?'

Calvin applied the truth so well to his times by claiming the papacy corrupted the true order of the church of God. He would have easily applied it in the same way today if he had been our contemporary, for there is corruption in our times about the true order of the church of God, even though it is plain to see in the New Testament what God has forbidden among His people in the way of public worship.

In further application, the man of Geneva tells us 'we are – with good reason – greatly exhorted to take thought of ourselves day and night, and to be vigilant to know how God wants to be worshipped and served'. *We are exhorted by him 'to apply all our powers to serve Him and are to bring back to memory things which we may have too quickly forgotten'.* He does not exaggerate when he tells us to recall the divine things with all our powers both day and night, for anything short of this will cause us to be victims of the kind of spiritual amnesia which takes hold of many believers.

Calvin in his consistency bids us 'carefully observe' what took place when Uzziah put out his hand to still the Ark; to 'study this passage carefully' where we see Uzziah mixing his fear with fantasies.

One of the fullest expositions on the need for clear thinking and good reasoning before God in Calvin's sermons on 2 Samuel is found in the twenty-fourth sermon, in which he deals with the incident concerning King David, after God has promised to build him a house by establishing the Davidic dynasty for the good of the people of Israel. David comes before God after the stupendous promise has been given and says, 'Who am I, eternal Lord, and what is my house that you have led me thus far?' Calvin's words on meditation are most memorable and deserve to be quoted in full:

Since our spirits are so flighty, we should be more careful than we are to apply ourselves on meditating on the works of God, for it is a study in which men are never sufficient in themselves. We hear what the Psalm 40 says, that if we applied ourselves to know how God governs us and how He disposes the condition of the human race, it would utterly surpass all our intelligence (Ps. 40:5). We could more easily count the hairs of our head a hundred times than understand the admirable providence of God as it really is. Thus if, on the one hand, we would carefully consider that God bestows such remarkable riches upon us in guiding and conducting us and, on the other, we would recognize that our spirits wander and are so feeble that they fail and faint, we would certainly take pains to meditate much more on the works of God.

As I said, we would remove every distraction, we would seek the means to help ourselves in order to elevate ourselves above the world. Then we would want to keep ourselves there, and avoid being immediately driven away, as has been our constant experience. But there are very few who do their duty in this matter as they should, so we must pay even more attention to this passage where it says that David, having heard the message which was brought to him by Nathan the prophet, 'entered in and sat down before the Lord' (2 Sam. 7:18). This was a sign he had chosen a secret place, and then he gave himself totally over to recognizing the benefits of God. He went down to the place where the Ark of the Covenant was placed, because the Holy Scripture calls it the face of God. The word implies that he sat down, but it should express the idea that he stopped, and that he entered not merely to rush through, but that he withdrew there for some time.

Therefore, we see how David, excellent man though he was, still knew the weakness of his spirit and, since he was a man, realized that he could be unstable – and, on the other hand, that he was helpless and worldly. For these two vices are in us: the one is that we are not able to understand the favours of God because we are wrapped up in our own worldly fantasies. Then the second is that although we have had a good beginning, it takes nothing to divert us, so that our spirits are scattered and wander hither and thither.[2]

Calvin says there is a place for public prayer, but there is a definite place for secret prayer as well, when meditation of the sincerest kind is more possible. In the company of others either our minds wander this way or that, or often ambition enters in so that we speak more to mortal creatures than to God. David went secretly to God to pray in a way that truly magnified God.

How could David magnify God best of all? By retreating from the company of others, 'to sharpen himself and elevate his senses above the world'. David had to persevere in this, in order to achieve the end of magnifying the favours of God according to their true merit, so he remained before God 'because this meditation required of him not only a minute, but it required his serious thought and his continuous examination of the words of God'.

With respect to meditating on the works of God in general, there is some benefit in this, as David shows in Psalm 8, when he thinks of the state of all men against the mercy of God, when he contemplates man's lack of worth in contrast to God's greatness.

Meditation requires us to be particular about these matters as it is not enough to recognize in general that we are nothing. To see the goodness of God in the most admirable way we must consider ourselves in particular. We must go from the 'What is man?' of Psalm 8 to the 'What am I?' of 2 Samuel. It is true that we can never understand and comprehend all of God's benefits – no amount of meditation could achieve such a feat – but we must attempt to take account of them.

Once again, Calvin talks of carefully thinking: 'When I have carefully thought and said: "I am nothing", and even when I have considered and closely watched and applied all my mental powers to commit to memory all that I have received...' In short,

2. *op. cit.*

we are to seek to comprehend the incomprehensible.

When it comes to taking note of all that God says, many of us find that what God says goes in one ear and out the other. Many are caught out by the stratagems of the devil. We are meant to study God's Word, never growing tired of doing so. Just as we keep eating in this life – after we have had dinner, then we have tea – we ought to have a continuous appetite for the things of God. Even if we are reproved, we ought not to be deterred from feeding on the Word. His word aids us in apprehending the power of God.

Yet we need more than understanding His power: 'We still need love and assurance quickly to enter into our hearts'. How can this come about? Through 'continual meditation, so that we know not only in passing what God declares to us but commit it to memory, so that when we pray to Him, we might seek to call on Him in such a way that He will never be far from us'. How we need to be fortified when it comes to keeping God's Word! It takes nothing to knock us down, says Calvin - 'as our experience proves too well'. Besides, the devil has spread his traps out everywhere to catch us, and the world is full of ambushes to catch us and bring us utterly down.

When Calvin comes to speaking of David being confronted by his sin through the straight word of Nathan the prophet, he shows us that David was a man who in his sin had become one whose faith 'was like a dying fire under the ashes'. Calvin causes us to see David failing to watch himself carefully by first becoming polygamous and we now readily witness the pitiful sight of one who foolishly had buried his memory and commits adultery. It points up the real need to keep our memory alive to the things of God.

The great mistakes in life are born out of simple decisions, and in the case of David is it too far-fetched to say that he came under the great heat of God's anger because he had not meditated? Of course, there is more to David feeling God's wrath because he buried his memory, as Calvin puts it, but just as small sparks can cause a great fire, so the failure to meditate can lead to sad consequences that seem all out of proportion to that first simple, secret and seeming-innocuous sin that gave rise to such a tragedy.

Calvin examines the mind of David after Nathan has pronounced 'You are the man!' and finds David pathetically blind to his own evil. Although knowing the difference between good and evil in general, David is witless when the case applies to him.

David is forgiven, but Calvin sees in the inspired record no guarantee that anyone who follows David will find mercy as David did. The case of David is frightening as we are reminded at the end of the sermon on Nathan rebuking the king, 'For there are so many things hidden in us, there are twisted thoughts, there are haughty affections, and God must uncover all of that'. *Is it not enough, dear reader, to drive us to a proper examination of ourselves, to prune our thoughts and desires, to follow carefully step by step the way of God?*

Still, it gives us heart to know that if those who are the elect of God ever commit such grievous sin, they can be awakened and made sensitive to their sin. Calvin, when preaching about David committing adultery, claims David had buried his memory, yes, 'totally buried his memory', but at the same time Calvin insists that David's faith was like a dying fire under the ashes prior to Nathan exposing his evil. He even says David had become totally corrupted when committing adultery, but he is careful to say: 'We see that, *for a time,* he (David) was totally corrupted ...'.

In essence, the Reformer is saying a believer contradicts himself when he turns to sin. This is so with David who is incensed when Nathan speaks the parable, thus proving he has 'some seed of the fear of God' in him. The expression *like a dying fire under the ashes* is not only a beautiful one employed by Calvin, but one that accurately defines the state of the backslidden believer. Therefore, we see how God in a single moment can make a believer feel his offences, and reveal that he as a believer is not dead at all.

Calvin does not mean David totally buried his memory in the strictest sense of the word. Calvin would not press the expression too hard; proof lies in his commentary on the king coming to his senses at Nathan's appearance. He says with respect to David, 'Thus, if they (believers) have been insensible, it is because the grace of God has been stifled by their ingratitude'. Perhaps Calvin could have said David's memory was totally buried *alive* for a little time in his sin. All the same, we know what Calvin means when he refers to total burial, and we know what he does not mean. David's memory was obviously not obliterated in the strict sense of the word when he sinned. What hurts at the appearance of Nathan is the memory of what God had graciously done for him and how he had shown his ingratitude by committing adultery. God brings to David's mind what he has been, what he ought to be. Here is the kind of meditation we dread – the kind that is forced upon us by the divine will to our sorrow.

And if we ever commit 'some huge and dreadful offence' as David committed, we are bidden to see it in terms of not just one evil committed – we are called to trace it back to our birth and acknowledge it 'as one of many sins stemming from the corruption in us since our birth'. This too calls for true self-examination.

God's way of dealing with sin

What of God forgiving David? What of the troubles that were to follow forgiveness? Had God truly forgiven him, or was the Lord saying he now must pay for his sins? Calvin, in a very moving passage on God chastising His children for their profit, with the threat of David losing his son in mind, claims God is not chastising David for the past but for the future. The chastisement is related to what happened in the past, but the past is forgiven. However, the past in a sense is remembered by the offender.

David is chastised for the future in that David has to be subdued even more. Forgiven, but 'so full of dishonesty, of refuse and wickedness that it is horrible'. We must be on our guard, and learn to hate our sin, and understand so as to make us walk much more carefully. Calvin finds the thought of God exacting payment from David abhorrent to the concept of forgiveness, but he insists David is being chastised in order 'to make him (David) more watchful, and to make him feel his evil more keenly, and think of it, instead of forgetting it'. If David had not been chastised and only forgiven, he would not have remembered the lesson so well.

Although Calvin does not say so, one can follow through and conclude that his sermons on David's sin and restoration show a perfect symmetry: David has it brought vividly to his mind in chastisement what he had stifled during his sin. If we believe God chastises His people appropriately, then we see how He will make the punishment fit the crime.

If we in our human judgment see wisdom in making the punishment fit the crime, how much more God! Therefore, what David sought to forget so adamantly in rebellion, he is made to remember with divine force in his restoration. May God spare us of that kind of meditation!

Meditation on Death

Now, to conclude with Calvin, a word about the letters he wrote, particularly those he wrote to prisoners who were on the point of dying for Christ.

Calvin himself wished for the discipline that shows a contempt for this present life as well as 'meditation of a holy death'. Therefore, he was able to write sympathetically to five prisoners who were incarcerated in Lyons in France.

The five prisoners had been declared guilty of heresy and delivered over to the secular arm of the Judge Ordinary of Lyons. In those times heresy in terms of false spiritual teaching was punishable by the secular government of the day in a number of countries where Roman Catholicism held sway. The Catholic Church believed she had authority over the spiritual and the secular and had the power to hand over to the state – supposedly the retributive arm of God – anyone who taught that which was contrary to Catholic teaching.

France, Calvin's homeland, was a Catholic country in 1553 when Calvin wrote from Geneva to encourage the five prisoners to be faithful to the cause of the gospel. The five had appealed to the Parliament of Paris but to no avail. The authorities of Berne, the Swiss Reformed city, sought to help the five but to no avail. Instead, they were taken from dungeon to dungeon during a trial which lasted for more than a year. At last they were returned to Lyons after being on trial in Paris, and on March 1st, 1553, they were told the Parliament had decided to burn them at the stake.

John Calvin writes with sympathy and yet with confidence to the five destined to die. He writes: 'Doubtless for a long time past you have meditated upon the last conflict which you will have to sustain, if it be His good pleasure to lead you thereto, and have even so fought hitherto that long practice has inured you to fill up what remains'. What does Calvin mean? He lived when many believers prized the value of serious meditation – such people lived in serious times – and he was certain that if the five had already been meditative when death had not been such an impinging threat, how much more meditative they would be when they knew death was near! Even when death had not been an impinging threat, like Calvin they would have prepared for death, as every Christian should, no matter what the circumstances are. The five would have spent in freer times many hours 'in meditation of a holy death'.

The 'long time past' that Calvin writes about to them doubtlessly refers to the trial that lasted for more than a year and which would have given rise to thoughts of dying by violence for the cause of Christ. Calvin is confident the five have meditated to the length whereby they have steeled themselves by the power of God to face martyrdom. 'If it be His good pleasure to lead you thereto' suggests the possibility of a reprieve, yet Calvin almost sees it as inevitable that the five will suffer at the cruel hands of the Inquisition. Furthermore, he knows one ought to prepare for not only what appears to be the inevitable, but for the worst.

He is confident they are ready to face the worst. Their meditation has been such that it can enable them to face the flames, as the 'long practice' of meditation has caused them in their holy imagination to see it through, if we may express it that way. Therefore, although he realises they will 'feel some twinges of frailty', he is confident in believing God will comfort them. God comforts those who are being chastised for their sins, how much more will He comfort them who are suffering innocently in their bid to champion the cause of trial?

For almost two months the five prisoners awaited the actual day of death. In the meantime the authorities of Berne had sought to have the sentence of death repealed, and perhaps Berne's attempted mediation prolonged the sentence. Anyhow, Calvin wrote to the five prisoners once again, only some days before the prisoners died.

He commends them for their willingness to die. While there was the hope of the sentence of death being repealed, it was right for them to seek such a hope. Yet, says Calvin, they were always fixing their mind on God when they were frustrated by any human hope. He writes:

> You have always settled on that firm foundation, even when it seemed as though you might be helped by men, and that we too thought so; but whatever prospect of escape you may have had by human means, *yet your eyes have never been dazzled so as to divert your heart and trust, either on this side or that.* Now at this present hour, necessity itself exhorts you more than ever to turn your whole mind heavenward.

Calvin continues on at some length to console those who will find it hard to suffer at the hands of those whose pride is 'so enormous', but he knows what their martyrdom will bring forth, while those who cruelly put them to death will one day suffer the horrible punishment prepared for such as have despised His majesty with 'such enormous pride'.

How difficult meditation is when one does not know whether a violent death is certain or not. Imagine the thoughts of those children of God who naturally wished to avoid such a death and yet it seemed inevitable. How the thoughts would turn this way and that! Hope and despair coming and going through their tormented minds.

Yet Calvin was confident that the five of Lyons never deviated from their conviction of being willing to die. For a time necessity did not compel them to think only of heaven. For a time there was hope. For a time there was the possibility of living on. For a time there was the possibility of being freed and there were hopeful thoughts about maintaining their witness to Christ in the world. There was room in their meditations for that. But the day of death is declared. No more can they dream of witnessing for Christ in the world. Now their whole mind, their entire mind is taken up with heaven.

When told that their day of death had come, the five received the news calmly. They cheerfully went to the stake singing psalms and recalling passages from God's Word. The youngest mounted the heap of wood first, the eldest last. The eldest made a request. The request was granted: he kissed the other four, saying to each one, 'Goodbye, goodbye, my brother'. The fire was lit. As the flames soared, all five exhorted one another, 'Courage, my brothers, courage...' until the flames overcame them.

Calvin wrote to other prisoners at Lyons some months after the five had met their cruel death, telling them as well they ought to meditate on the celestial glory and immortality that the Son of God purchased so dearly for us.

Then he wrote to a brother of Admiral Coligny when he had recanted upon pressure. Calvin wrote tenderly and yet with some degree of admonishment when he told him that he should have 'duly considered the matter with a closer scrutiny'. Calvin did not write in effect 'You have done what I would not have done,' but put the emphasis on what the right thinking of any believer requires. Did he emphasize that recanting occurs because we have not considered the matter at all? No, that rather it occurs when we have not considered it under close scrutiny. He bids his brother in Christ to have thought for the honour of God and says poignantly: 'Nay, if we reflect on the shortness of life, it ought not to cost us much to follow our Lord Jesus to His death and burial in order to be partakers of His glory.'

As we consider how we would have fared in those perilous times of Calvin, if we conclude he was rightfully encouraging the five but was rather harsh to the recanter, remember Calvin knew he appeared harsh to the recanter. But he knew as well that every believer must think things through, in the light of God's Word and glory, of being faithful to our God whose honour ought to be our chief concern.

7

ROBERT MURRAY M'CHEYNE

Robert Murray M'Cheyne (1813–1843) died at the age of twenty-nine, and yet it can be claimed that few preachers of the gospel[1] have greatly influenced their own and succeeding generations in so short a life. Indeed, his brief ministry of seven and a half years at St. Peter's, Dundee, Scotland, achieved more that will last for eternity than most accomplish in a lifetime.

He was born in Edinburgh in May, 1813, the youngest of five. His father was a prosperous lawyer. When M'Cheyne went to university at the age of fourteen to do an Arts degree, he gained a number of prizes for being an exceptional student in all the classes he attended. He had had a Christian background when young – once at the age of five or six surprising some friends with his ability to recite fluently passages of Scripture by heart – but at university he whiled away his hours playing cards (remember people in those days were often addicted to squandering an inordinate number of hours doing it), dancing and gymnastics, all without a care for his soul.

Then the death of his eldest brother, David, shocked him into considering eternity, as his brother had been an exemplary believer. It was then that Robert began to seek 'a Brother who cannot die'. He became serious in contrast to the levity of spending life in Edinburgh's fashionable places, and began to sit

---

1. Two volumes of M'Cheyne's sermons are available from Christian Focus Publications. *From The Preacher's Heart* is a hardback edition of a volume originally entitled 'Additional Remains of the Rev. Robert Murray M'Cheyne'. It contains 64 sermons and 15 lectures. *A Basket of Fragments* is a large format paperback containing an additional 37 sermons.

under an evangelical ministry. He was eighteen at the time of his brother's death and he surprised his friends with his acquired gravity. It seems his conversion was somewhat gradual and he came to Christ through deep and abiding convictions, particularly experiencing an indelible impression of the pollution of his nature. He saw that original sin was the cause of all his actual sins. Through this he turned to God and eagerly sought His grace. In 1831 he entered the divinity hall of the university.

In 1836 he began his ministry at St Peter's, in a new church in what was a sadly neglected district of some 4,000 people. At the outset his congregation amounted to about 1,100 hearers – a spiritually dead place but a wide field for labour.

M'Cheyne began his ministry by first drawing men's attention to the truth that mankind is lost in sin. He believed that sinners needed to feel deeply for their sin in order to want the Saviour. His preaching met with great success. Statistics cannot be given as to how many were converted in his ministry, since the great man lived in an age when devout men were not concerned with numbers, believing conversion is a work of the sovereign God, and that there was too much presumption made about those who respond to the gospel. It was characteristic in M'Cheyne's time to describe people at least for a time as *hopefully* saved. Still, the growing number of communicants were recorded and this gives us some idea of the success M'Cheyne knew among the people. The town knew in his first years of ministry that they had a unique man of God amongst them, though he was also a sick man all that time.

Prolonged illness caused some to think that their pastor would gain from visiting Palestine, as it was thought the climate there would help heal him. So in the spring of 1839 he went to study the possibility of a mission to the Jews. He said, 'We should be like God in his peculiar affections; and the whole Bible shows

God has ever had and still has, a peculiar love to the Jews.' He held the view God has a special love for both the land of Israel and the people of Israel. He took the Old Testament prophecies about Israel literally. Even in the land of Palestine, he never forgot his people back home and at one time wrote to them: 'If you tread the glorious gospel of grace under your feet, your souls will perish; and I fear Dundee one day will be a howling wilderness like Capernaum.'

Not long after the party turned homewards through Asia Minor, M'Cheyne was taken dangerously ill and he felt he would die. As he lay near Smyrna gravely ill, he was praying for the people at St. Peter's. On one of those days as he was praying thus, a wonderful revival broke out in Dundee under W. C. Burns, just as it had broken out in Kilsyth under the same man. We are told that in the revival 'tears were streaming from the eyes of many, and some fell on the ground groaning, and weeping, and crying for mercy'. Services were held every night for many weeks – often lasting till late hours. The fear of God so fell upon the town that people came in droves to fill the churches. M'Cheyne returned to Dundee to witness unforgettable scenes of people 'praising a present God'.

Revival accompanied M'Cheyne as well after he returned to Scotland. He became known all over Scotland, not only preaching in churches, but out in the open air where he attracted thousands to hear him, whether under a star-spangled sky or in pouring rain.

All the same, he was an ill young man. In his twenty-ninth year he became increasingly conscious of the brevity of time:

I do not expect to live long .... Changes are coming; every eye before me shall soon be dim in death. Another pastor shall feed this flock; another singer lead the psalm; another flock shall fill this fold... There is no believing, no repenting, no conversion in the grave – no minister will speak to you there. This is the time

of conversion. Oh! my friends, you have no ordinances in hell
– there will be no preaching in hell .... Oh that you use this little
time! Every moment of it is worth a world.

In the February of his last year, despite illness, he went to the
northwest of Scotland, preaching twenty-seven times in twenty-
four different places, often travelling through heavy snow. On
March 12th back in Dundee he preached his final sermon. In the
week to follow a burning fever came on him until he became
delirious. He died March 24th, 1843.

What made M'Cheyne great? We know that the world often
accords fame to those who die prematurely, but is there more to
M'Cheyne's life than it being short-lived? It pays investigation.

A Life of Discipline

Even as a student in preparation for the ministry, M'Cheyne did
not while away his time in unprofitable things, but showed
himself to be one who was destined to do great deeds for Christ.
His own spiritual growth, which would lead to much fruitfulness
in the ministry, revolved around a strict daily programme of
Bible study, prayer and meditation. He was tempted in the early
stages of his divinity course to retreat at times to fashionable
pleasures of the world, but it was with 'growing alarm' as
Andrew Bonar his noted biographer tells us.

Ever mindful of his brother's premature death, and his own
illnesses, M'Cheyne, with a fellow student, set on a course to
improve his spiritual welfare. Both of them met together for
study of the Scriptures, for prayer and for serious conversation.
They also 'watched each other's steps in the narrow way'. A
diary was kept for recording spiritual experiences. Also some of
the students banded together for the purpose of setting apart an
hour or two every week for visiting people in the neglected parts
of the town. The visits that M'Cheyne made with others im-

pressed upon him 'the sinner's depravity in all its forms'. *Such visits drove him to speak of Christ to others,* but *he knew the peril of neglecting his own soul, yes, even in the busyness of doing those things spiritually profitable. He would lament: 'Private meditation exchanged for conversation.* Here is the root of the evil – forsake God and He forsakes us.'

In his early years of life at divinity college, his studies did not absorb his whole attention, but as time moved on he took to them more seriously, realizing that he was forming the character for a future ministry. He told another student: 'If you acquire slovenly or sleepy habits of study now, you will never get the better of it. Do everything in its own time. Do everything in earnest - if it is worth doing, then do it with all your might. Above all, keep much in the presence of God. Never see the face of any man till you have seen His face who is our life, our all.'

To another he reminded him to beware of overly-studying the classics lest he become less inclined towards the things of God. He said the classics were like the poisons chemists handle, 'poisons that need studying for their qualities but handled with care'. Even in summer vacations some of the young men, including M'Cheyne, sought to 'redeem the time' with profitable study together. Anyone who has ever been a theological student and has known the pitfalls of idling away the hours with fellow students in things not all that edifying, will understand that M'Cheyne was showing an uncommon maturity for one aspiring to be a preacher of the Word.

He became familiar with the works of Jonathan Edwards, the great American philosopher-theologian-preacher of the eighteenth century, and adopted some of Edwards' practices to become more spiritually alive. For instance, he adopted the idea of making up spiritual resolutions to follow. These are some of the things he resolved to do:

Resolved never to lose one moment of time but to improve it in the
most profitable way I can.
Resolved that I will live so as I had wished I had done when I had
come to die.
Resolved to live with all my might while I do live ....

At the end of the college days M'Cheyne recorded in his diary:
'College finished Friday last. My last appearance there. Life
itself is vanishing fast, make haste for eternity.'

Thus, when he began his ministry at St Peter's, Dundee, in
November, 1836, he began as a man most conscious of eternity.
How did he maintain his consciousness of eternity? His concern
for his own soul and his dread of others going to hell came about
primarily through the cultivation of his own spirit. He wrote to
a fellow minister:

> Your own soul is your first and greatest care. Seek advance of
> personal holiness. It is not great talents God blesses so much as
> great likeness to Jesus. A holy minister is an awful weapon in
> the hand of God. A word spoken by you when your conscience
> is clear, and your heart's full of the Holy Spirit, is worth ten
> thousand words spoken in unbelief and sin.

Love of the Word

His mind was occupied much with the Scriptures. Like the
Puritan, John Owen, M'Cheyne believed we ought to spend the
best hours of the day in communion with God, not when we are
tired and our mind has been heavily taxed with other things. He
found his morning hours from six to eight o'clock the most
uninterrupted. After tea was a good hour as well. When people
were criticizing ministers for not being public enough in the
sense of visiting, etc., M'Cheyne hit back at the criticism with the
words: '...they cry that ministers should be more in public; they
think that it is an easy thing to interpret the Word of God, and to

preach. But a minister's duty is not so much public as private.'

Before breakfast he often sang to himself a Psalm of praise. Then he usually read three chapters of the Word, though he never thought it was enough. *He meditated on the Word until it came powerfully to his own heart. At the beginning of his ministry, three passages of Scripture particularly arrested him: Isaiah 26:3, 1 Timothy 4:15 and Isaiah 6:8. He applied such Scriptures to his forthcoming ministry, and as he meditated he trembled.*

Mingled with the reading of the Word was prayer. M'Cheyne got his thoughts and words from God, took them, applied them to his heart, and sent up prayer that those thoughts and words may be his in holy living. Occasionally, in addition to regular prayer, he set apart time for more sustained prayer as well as fasting. At times in the early years he would ride out in the afternoon to a ruined church, where he enjoyed an hour's solitude in prayer and solemn meditation.

Prior to preaching he spent time in prayer. He endeavoured to get to bed early Saturday night to get up early Sunday morning. His sermons having already been drawn up, he engaged in prayer for his hearers in the early hours of Sunday.

He also felt prayer and meditation was the forerunner to successful visitation of his flock. What can often be pedestrian if not done with all the heart, became a profitable time for the young preacher. He was to say in regard to visiting: 'It is a great thing to be furnished by meditation and prayer before setting out; it makes you a far more full and faithful witness.'

M'Cheyne always favoured the reading of solid spiritual books, especially those written by the Puritans, but it was in the Scriptures that he found the choicest food for his soul. This conviction he passed on to young people. On a blank sheet for a little boy in his congregation he once wrote:

> Love your Bible more than play –
> Grow in wisdom every day.

Soon after he arrived at St. Peter's he began a prayer meeting on a Thursday evening, though it was not confined to prayer. He first gave the people on those nights 'a Scripture to be hidden in the heart', which he followed up with a twenty minute exposition on the passage of Scripture to be hidden, usually it being a passage of Scripture relating to the promise of the Spirit or the effects of the outpouring of the Spirit. This was calculated to awaken his people's interest in revival, and was tied in with his reading of some history of revival. For a time on Thursday nights in 1838, in his third year in the pastorate, he did a series on the Letters to the Seven Churches, and the series proved a blessing to many, some of whom came from a considerable distance to be there. M'Cheyne held that prayer must be based on a knowledge of God's Word, and excited by what God has done through the centuries in bringing revival and the outpouring of His Spirit.

It takes a strong man to exercise discipline in the church, and one feels that only a strong inner conviction coming from such meditation made M'Cheyne able to carry it out – indeed, not only to carry it out, but use it as a means of conversion to not a few.

With respect to the Lord's Supper, he perceived that it was the New Testament rule for anyone with 'a credible profession' to share in the Supper, even if he as the minister might have had some doubts about the person; but he was strong in his insistence of not allowing any unconverted people to come to the Lord's Table. When communicants came for the first time, he would ask them if their souls were saved. His straightforward dealings with some flippant young people led to their conversion. He admitted that when he first went to St. Peter's, he was 'ignorant of the vast importance of church discipline'. He thought his work simply was to pray and preach.

When cases of discipline were brought before him and the elders, he 'regarded them with something like abhorrence'. He so feared the exercising of discipline that he nearly gave up the ministry. Yet he went ahead and practised it, and found to his pleasure it could be the means of conversion. He realised this most important truth at last: '...if preaching be an ordinance of Christ, so is church discipline'. He came to regard preaching and discipline to be two keys: preaching is the key by which the treasures of the Scriptures are unlocked, while discipline is the key by which we open or close the way to the sealing ordinances of the faith.

Only a man who has practised the presence of God seriously can ever behave as did M'Cheyne. He was ever conscious that one idle word, one needless contention, one covetous act might undo all his good work of solemn exhortation and earnest warning, church discipline not excepted, therefore he spent much time in privately examining himself and elevating himself on the thoughts and the ways of God as they appear in His holy Word.

He also wanted to be to others in private what he was in public. He knew men can tolerate preaching against their sins publicly through a sermon, as long as the preacher is easy with them once he has descended the pulpit and lives as they do, and talks as they talk. He aspired to say the same things to men face-to-face that he would say in the pulpit – and with the same earnestness. He always wished to guide the conversation to things of eternity when he was in company outside the church – if he could not, he would remain silent. He took it as a rule that when one visits a company of people and there are strangers in the company, one ought to turn the conversation to the things of eternity, as more than likely God has brought any stranger into your midst providentially for his salvation. Despite his ailing condition, as a true man of God he availed himself of any opportunity that arrived for the gospel's sake, not wishing to procrastinate. 'Surely – what do we live for?'

Bonar says that M'Cheyne became so ill that he could not continue with his work at Dundee without having a break. Yet the period of rest which M'Cheyne was compelled to take was the means by which God continued to bless the people at St. Peter's, at a time when they had come to idolizing their preacher. *M'Cheyne himself confessed round about that time: 'Often God does not bless us when we are in the midst of our labours lest we should say, "My hand and my eloquence has done it."* He removes us in silence and then pours down a blessing so that there is no room to receive it.'

M'Cheyne believed that by going to Palestine he would be contributing to the evangelization of the Jews, in the hope that God would pour out His Spirit on them and thus pour out His blessing on the Gentiles as a consequence. His first contact with a Jew occurred on the ship which carried him to England at the beginning of the journey to Palestine. The Jew did not wish to be identified as a son of Abraham. M'Cheyne took out his Hebrew Bible and read with him Psalm 1 in Hebrew, and pressed home that duty which was so dear to the heart of the young man himself – the duty of meditating on the Word of the Lord.

Love of the Old Testament

The prospect of going to Palestine excited M'Cheyne, as he had a love for all of God's Word, the Old Testament as well as the New. It is said he especially loved the types found in the Old Testament and the plain text of the New.

It is somewhat revelatory to discover that such a man as M'Cheyne, with a burning desire to see men saved, would spend time on what many regard as the obscure parts of the Word. It would be surprising to many a modern to learn that such a man spent time in what appears as a somewhat barren part of the Old Testament and then wrote a poem to memorize what that part of the Old Testament contains. The part in mind is Numbers 4, where one reads about the way God ordered the Ark of the Covenant and the equipment of the sanctuary to be carried as the Israelites travelled in the desert, and how the Levites were made responsible for carrying the whole equipment and which of the clans were to carry the various articles as they journeyed. Here is the poem M'Cheyne composed in order to memorize what Numbers 4 tells us:

> The Kohathites upon their shoulder bear
> The holy vessels, covered with all care;
> The Gershonites receive an easier charge,
> Two waggons full of cords and curtains large;
> Merari's sons four ponderous waggons load
> With boards and pillars of the house of God.

Says Bonar: 'He acted on the principle that whatever God has revealed must deserve our study and prayerful investigation.'

Many of us pay lip service to such a statement as Bonar's, for how many of us deep down truly believe that every part of the Scriptures is useful to us? We all find great blessing in the New Testament where Christ is spoken about plainly, and some find particular parts of the Old Testament edifying (particularly the Psalms), but how many would gain any benefit from such a portion as Numbers 4?

Do not many of us actually play down the importance of the Old Testament and think we could survive on the New Testament alone if somehow the Old Testament suddenly disappeared and we had lost our opportunity to read it? Is not there still some vestiges of the teaching of Marcion[2] in our midst?

---

2. Marcion was a second century heretic in Rome, who propagated the notion that the God of the Old Testament, while not exactly an evil being, was not good in the sense of the Father of Jesus, the God of love and grace.

Perhaps one of the difficulties arises from the names we have given to the two major parts of the Bible – the Old and New Testaments, we call them. Perhaps Adolph Saphir, a discerning Christian Jew who became a Presbyterian minister in Scotland, and later a missioner to his own people as well as to Gentiles in Europe, had it right when he claimed we ought to rename the two parts and call them The Book of Israel and The Book of the Church. He would never have professed that such names were watertight in terms of definition, but he saw them as a marked improvement on the present names, names that cause believers and others to dismiss the Old Testament because it is reckoned as 'old' and therefore inferior in terms of inspiration.

M'Cheyne certainly viewed the Old Testament in a practical sense as The Book of Israel, believing it contained many prophecies made about literal Israel which, when they come true, will reveal Israel upon being converted as the means of blessing to the whole world. Saphir's approach lends itself to an unbreakable unity between the two testaments and reveals the two testaments simply from two angles or emphases with regard to the salvation of mankind.

Be that as it may, can we imagine some of our modern-day evangelists exploring the Scriptures in the way the zealous and successful evangelist of Dundee did, and storing such seemingly-obscure knowledge to ruminate on? Is it unkind to caricature the contemporary evangelist as one who is acquainted with a few random New Testament texts that are used over and over, preaching with material that mainly is derived outside of the Word in the form of newspaper clippings, anecdotes, stories strong on the subjective to pull at the heart-strings? One feels that listening to such men once or twice is sufficient since ensuing sermons or messages will simply regurgitate what was said before. It was not so with M'Cheyne. Someone once asked if he was afraid of running short of sermons, to which he replied: 'No, I am just an interpreter of Scripture in my sermons; and when the Bible runs dry, I shall.'

Says Bonar: 'He (M'Cheyne) endeavoured at all times to preach the mind of the Spirit in a passage.' He was afraid of grieving the Spirit. Believing all is the Word of God and all is inspired by the same Spirit, he ventured forth to use many parts of the Old Testament as well as the New. It seems strange to some people that an evangelist should adopt such a stance, particularly if they view an evangelist as being distinct from a pastor or a teacher.

It may be difficult to ascertain from Bonar's biography whether M'Cheyne was more of an evangelist than a teacher, if one likes such distinctions. Yet he undoubtedly was an evangelist and a pastor, and he possessed the kind of biblical knowledge many a contemporary believer would acknowledge as essential for a sound and profound Bible teacher. Whatever distinctions we may like to hold, M'Cheyne was a successful evangelist with enduring fruit and one who firmly believed no part of God's Word ought to escape the believing eye.

It can be presumed that such a poem as M'Cheyne drew up about the Levites carrying the articles of the sanctuary was not simply composed to recall who did what. It stands that the young minister of Dundee would have employed all his power to apply such knowledge to his heart. We are not informed as to how he applied it, but it is interesting that upon the heels of reference to the actual words of M'Cheyne's poem on the Levites, Bonar adds that sentence: 'He acted on the principle that whatever God has revealed must deserve our study and prayerful consideration.'

Admittedly, to apply the facts of Numbers 4 is more difficult than applying much of the New Testament, and it takes a skilled man to do it, but it can be done, as God has revealed such things in his Word to be applied. M'Cheyne claimed, God has given us

His Spirit, and in *prayerful* meditation we can gain light.

M'Cheyne took with him to Palestine some notes on Leviticus which his biographer-to-be, Andrew Bonar, had drawn up. Since he knew Bonar well, and since Andrew Bonar's commentary on Leviticus has proved to be an enduring and insightful commentary, one can assume M'Cheyne drew such inspiration from the ability Bonar possessed to apply the more so-called obscure parts of Scripture.

When the ailing but adored preacher went to Palestine, Andrew Bonar saw his friend at close inspection and found him to be a true man of God. 'Holiness in him was manifested, not by efforts to perform duty, but in a way so natural, that you recognized therein the easy outflowing of the indwelling Spirit.'

The Priority of Prayer

Even in a far-off country, and despite being ill as he underwent some difficult travelling, M'Cheyne never forgot prayer and meditation. Especially at Mount Olivet he felt a divine presence. Although Bonar's brother had said to M'Cheyne before he left Scotland that the spiritual world holds more promise than any place in this physical world, M'Cheyne knew that Mt. Olivet at least was a physical place that helps one discover divine things. There at its foot, Gethsemane moved him to think deeply on Christ's love to undergo divine wrath for us. There nearby was the spot where Jesus wept over the city, revealing His human tenderness as well as His superhuman love. There to the southeast lay Bethany, reminding him of Lazarus being raised from the dead and of the hope of the future resurrection. From there he could see the Dead Sea, the area where God rained down fire and brimstone on Sodom and Gomorrah, the cities reminding him of judgment reserved for all who neglect God's salvation. And everywhere he went, his people of Dundee were also in his thoughts and prayers.

When he returned to Dundee, his people welcomed him 'with the greatest joy'. The road to his home was crowded with young and old. He had to shake hands with many at the same time. Before the crowd dispersed, they pressed him to speak some words of life to them and to pray with them where they stood. When he finally reached home, he was to exclaim, 'To Your name, O Lord, be all the glory!'

Upon his return, encouraged by the revival that was sweeping through many parts of Scotland, he preached in places other than Dundee, as the Spirit came down and revealed to men the beauty of Christ and the hardness of their hearts in lingering to love Him who gave Himself so sacrificially. He even went to Ireland to preach.

In the latter time of his ministry, however, when he was 'exposed to several attacks of illness, experienced some severe personal trials, and felt the assaults of sore temptation', he received an invitation to preach in various places, including the open air, in northern England.

It was a troubled time for him as far as the flock of Dundee was concerned, for some complained about M'Cheyne being absent too much from what they considered his regular pulpit. Yet he felt he was being called more to evangelistic than pastoral labours at that stage of his life. Whenever he returned to his flock, he fell into discouragement, believing God was not blessing his ministry as formerly. Therefore, one day he took to walking in the fields. What happened? Let us read his own words:

> As I was walking through the fields, the thought came over me with overwhelming power, that everyone of my flock must soon be in heaven or hell. O how I wished I had a tongue like thunder, that I might make all hear; or that I had a frame like iron, that I might visit everyone, and say, 'Escape for your life!' Ah, sinners! You little know how I fear that you will lay the blame of your damnation at my door.

He feared he would become proud of his own holiness, and so from this time on he wrote down for his own benefit an examination of things in his life that had to be amended or changed. He was not sated with what some may call success; rather like Ignatius of old, he thought, 'It is only now that I begin to be a disciple'.

He called his written record of personal examination *Reformation*. Bonar categorizes (or did M'Cheyne himself?) the examination into two parts: (1) Personal reformation; (2) Reformation in prayer.

Personal Reformation

What occupied M'Cheyne's mind as he sought personal reformation? He determined to be as perfect in holiness as it is possible to be on earth, and any voice in his mind telling him the contrary he declared to be of the devil.

He resolved to rid his mind radically of sin. He felt he should confess his sins more often, in fact, confess them as soon as they are committed, no matter where he happened to be, lest he added sin to sin. He desired a short account with God, but if anything prevented him from achieving that, then he set times for confessing sin in the nearest convenient hour. He endeavoured to confess his sins after breakfast and after tea. This was not to be easy as he knew the devil sought to frustrate him, that by dwelling on the sin confessed the devil would not let the chance slip by to remind him that he would commit that sin again sometime in the future, or that the sin was not actually forgiven. He sought to confess all the sins of his life, raking up what he had done in his youth and so on.

In the light of the rigours of God's law he hoped to bring forward every dream, every 'floating thought', every predilection, all recurring actions, all habits of thought and feeling and action, to look seriously at every slander of his enemies lest such slander had truth in it, every reproof or bantering that friends levelled at him lest there was some truth in anything they said, and all traces of prevailing sin. He thought that for more searching examination a day should be spent, perhaps once a month, in fasting. Adversity in the form of physical illness, domestic problems, problems in the house or the church, were to be viewed seriously. Even the sins and adversity of others were seen as God calling on him to confess his own sins. Especially near the time to preach did the ailing pastor feel the need to confess his sins.

Confessing sin was only part of his personal reformation. M'Cheyne had forgiveness in mind and the desire to be filled of the Holy Spirit. Every sin, no matter how small it appeared, must be washed away through the blood of Christ. Being ashamed ought not to deter one from seeking such a cleansing, for it is God's way for peace and holiness. Neither are any sins too great to be cleansed. In fact, the weight of heavy sins should act like the weight of a grandfather clock – the heavier it is, the faster it goes – and should compel one to go to Christ more quickly. Go to Christ, who not only cleanses from sin, but clothes us with His righteousness through the true obedience He attained, that obedience which becomes ours.

When that is done, the filling of the Holy Spirit is necessary as well. Gunpowder is ever dangerous when it is dry, and it has no inherent property to help it resist fire, so the believer, as soon as the Spirit leaves him, he, like dry gunpowder, is open to and becomes helpless to temptation. No matter for how long one has been a believer, no matter how experienced he may be, sin can flare up. 'If I would be filled with the Spirit, I feel I must read the Bible more, pray more and watch more.'

To confess sin, be cleansed by Christ and clothed with His righteousness, to be filled by the Spirit, all speaks of the happiness that is inseparably linked with holiness. M'Cheyne saw God has never sinned yet He has happiness. Christ never sinned yet He has happiness. The redeemed in heaven will never sin for all eternity and yet they will be happy. The Devil tempts, 'Why not enjoy the pleasure of sin? You still may go to heaven.' 'No,' said M'Cheyne, 'my true happiness is to go and sin no more.' Sin must be shunned and instead of thinking or entertaining evil, 'I ought to meditate often on heaven as a world of holiness – where all are holy, where the joy is holy joy, the work holy work; so that, without personal holiness, I can never be there ... I ought to avoid the appearance of evil. God commands me; and I find that Satan has a singular art in linking the appearance and reality together.' Satan is subtle; even speaking about some sins defiles one, so does seeing evil, so may the notion of believing that some evil things are necessary to know in order to help pastor people. *'I am persuaded that nothing is thriving in my soul unless it is growing.'*

With respect to reformation in prayer, M'Cheyne ached to be engaged especially in more secret, private prayer, the kind of prayer that should include at least once a day confession of sin, adoration, thanksgiving and intercession. He lamented that frequently he rose and it was well into the day before he was in secret prayer. Family prayer, corporate prayer does not take its place; indeed, such prayer is soured by secret prayer having not been practised. He strove ever to make good the following rule: seek God's face first each day before seeing anyone else's face.

Do we think we moderns are the busiest people who have ever existed? Then take note of these words: 'If I have slept too long, or am going on an early journey, or my time is in any way shortened, it is best to dress hurriedly, and have a few minutes alone with God, than give it up for lost'. He says it is best to spend at least one hour alone with God before engaging in anything else. The best hours are to be spent in communion with God – for M'Cheyne the best were six to eight in the morning and after tea, as has already been mentioned.

Prayer should be employed at all times, even when one wakes up in the night. And prayer must feed on the Word; for M'Cheyne it meant reading three chapters of Scripture each day, with Sunday morning spent looking over the chapters read during the week and taking particular note of the verses he had marked. With regard to the three daily chapters, he felt they should come from three different places in the Bible. (M'Cheyne made up a Bible reading calendar to enable believers to read the Bible in a whole year. It was designed for families as well as individuals. This calendar is still being used by many people today. He called the calendar *Daily Bread*.)

M'Cheyne, whose body was racked by a number of illnesses, became greatly exposed to typhoid fever, which was rampant in his city as he neared the end of his life here on earth. Right to the end he preached, exhorted and encouraged. In fact, near the end, in a space of three weeks he had preached or spoken at twenty-four different places. He who once said 'Live so as to be missed' suddenly died and hundreds of people gathered at the church to mourn. Hearts were bursting with grief. When he came to be buried, the shops were closed all around, and great crowds lamented his loss.

The Balanced Man
What do we make of Robert Murray M'Cheyne? Or, more frighteningly perhaps, what would he make of us? Some may say he was somewhat legalistic, though we must remember that his resolutions and practices are things found in his diary and not in sermon notes for public instruction. Still, is there anything we can learn from him?

Some may desire the zeal he possessed – and what spiritually sane believer would not? But they may question the way by which he kept his zeal burning. For instance, it may be thought he overdid it when it came to confessing his sins.

Well, we must ask ourselves: what is exactly meant by confession of sins? If we take a passage such as 1 John 1:9, what does it mean exactly? Does it mean what M'Cheyne thought it meant? It really comes down to this: do we confess our sins by being general or do we confess them by being particular? The Scripture, it may be said, as related to 1 John 1:9, explicitly bids us to do neither.

Yet have we truly confessed our sins if we have not been particular? Is it sufficient, for instance, in the evening hours to admit only, 'Lord, forgive me of my sin today?' Or even to admit, 'Lord, forgive me for any act of jealousy?' Is it not more profitable to track down any actual times of jealousy? If Christ's forgiveness merely means a soothing word of forgiveness, then perhaps general confession could be adequate, but one must remember Christ more than speaks a word of forgiveness – in the past He shed His blood to forgive. As Christians we must never forget that. Yes, He died for our actual sins, those sins we commit from day to day, therefore we should name those actual sins.

One can hear the modern voice, 'What about my self-esteem? Will not the cross shatter it?' Yes, it will, but will it be to the slaying of you as a person? No, only as a slaying of your sin. You remain as a person, one loved of God, forgiven of God, one desperately feeling his need of the Spirit in order to overcome sin and have fellowship with God.

There ought to be no fear of being a victim of 'psychological battering' at the cross, like some so-called Christian leaders fear. If we spend our time confessing all our actual sins, the enormity of them will overwhelm us, yet the enormity ought not to drive us to despair. There is no sense in which M'Cheyne habitually despaired when he miscroscopically looked at his evil, as he did not linger in such matters. M'Cheyne actually knew all that modern Christian psychologists fear, only he saw it in terms of the devil 'making use of the confession of sin to stir up again the very sin confessed into new exercise, so that I am afraid to dwell upon the confession'. He confessed he needed the help of experienced Christians in regard to this matter, but at the same time he contended that the devil was trying to drive him away from confessing and he ought to be resisted lest there is an 'awful abuse of confession'. We must ask ourselves: which is the most awful thing of all, to confess or not to confess? Anyone who has a clear notion of God knows the answer. So too did John, who wrote that we ought not sin, but if we do, then we have Someone to speak in our defence – Jesus Christ, the Righteous One.

M'Cheyne, who died deliriously but saying: 'I'll tell you what I like, faithfulness to God and a holy walk', was one who agonized over himself and over others with regard to salvation, yet his agony was accompanied by holy joy. Agony and joy may seem contrary to the world – indeed, even for many Christians today – but according to the Word of God, the two are not in conflict. While we are in this world agony over our sin ought to be ours, but for the people of God, godly sorrow brings repentance that leads to salvation and leaves no regret. We will be happy when our sorrow leads to repentance (see 2 Corinthians 7:8–10).

M'Cheyne was a balanced man. With those who have the glory of God in mind, we may say, 'Let us have his imbalance rather than the "balance" of many others.' He preached as he lived – living and preaching 'the certainties of eternal life with an undoubting mind'. Do we need anything more? Can we afford anything less?

8

JOHN NEWTON

Newton (1725–1807) is particularly remembered these days as the author of the hymn *Amazing Grace,* and as the young man involved in the African slave trade and who, on boarding a ship headed for England, was arrested by the Spirit of God in a violent storm on the ocean, which experience led to his amazing conversion. To others, who know a little more about Newton, he is remembered as the successful minister of the Gospel, first at Olney and then at Woolnoth in London. To others, who are even more acquainted with him, Newton is, as Marcus Loane once described him, 'the letter writer *par excellence* of the Evangelical Revival [of the eighteenth century]'.

It is in his letters we come to the soul of the former slave trader and find one who has much to tell us about the nature of man, which contemplative study consumed much of Newton's time and made him the great man he was.

John Newton was born in London in 1725. His mother was a devout Christian but died before John's seventeenth birthday. His stern father was a man of the sea. He took John with him when his son was only eleven, making six voyages with him. As a godless young fellow, he was one day press-ganged. He hated the life on the ship and soon deserted it, only to be captured two days later. Newton was severely punished. Soon after he was put on board a slave ship bound for Africa. After a humiliating experience on the coast of Sierra Leone, his life fluctuated between being master of slave ships and being a poorly paid seaman.

After being wonderfully converted, Newton, strange though

it may seem, became master of a slave ship before he turned surveyor at Liverpool and eventually became a minister of the Gospel.

In his studies prior to entering the ministry, Newton used to combine the searching of the Scriptures with reading of the classics, but he came to the conviction that life was too short to give even a part of his time to the classics. 'Neither poet nor historian could tell me a word of Jesus; and I therefore applied myself to those who could.' He neatly divided every day into three lots of eight hours: eight hours for sleep, eight hours for exercise and devotion, eight hours to his books.

Newton enjoyed a long and very useful ministry. He was still preaching at the age of eighty, asking 'What! Shall the old African blasphemer stop while he can speak?' To the end of his days he remained a shrewd observer of human nature, as well as an able exponent of the Word. He used to say, 'A man, wherever he is, should always be in his study. He should look at every man, and at everything, as capable of affording him some instruction.'

Josiah Bull once said Newton is to be remembered more for his goodness than his greatness. It depends on wherein lies his greatness. Newton might not have been learned in the more abstract and scholastic niceties of the theological arguments, but in the knowledge of God's Word, in the knowledge of the human heart with all its wants and weaknesses, few have excelled him. Strictly speaking, it may not be correct to say the former slave trader turned his back on the theological niceties – as he might have been capable of reaching considerable intellectual heights – but it is true to say he viewed such matters as unimportant points in preference for what is of great moment for the souls of men.

His success as a pastor lay in 'his capacity and habit of entering into [his hearers'] trials and experiences ...'.

Newton the Counsellor

Newton wrote hundreds of letters as a counsellor, his collection *Cardiphonia* ('Voice of the Heart') being the most widely-known. He certainly regarded *Cardiphonia* as his most useful collection of writings. So did others, who returned letters to him so they might be printed. As someone has said: '[In his letters] you feel that you are listening to a man who is telling you what he himself has seen, and felt, and tasted of the goodness of that God, whose Word and service he commends'. Newton simply did not bid his readers to possess feelings of comfort and joy – he, in the spirit of the infallible writers of Scriptures, always gave sound and solid objective reasons for comfort and joy. We are always sure when reading Newton's illuminating letters why he writes what he does. And much of the success of his easy-to-read letters lies in the fruit of his solid contemplation of the truths of God.

In some forty-one letters which he wrote, and which have been classified as 'Forty-one Letters on Religious Subjects,' Newton, in response to those who sought him for counsel, often wrote about meditation.

One who sought his counsel, for instance, was a theological student. The student was warned by Newton to beware of becoming unspiritual in college days. Says Newton, 'Although I am no enemy to the acquisition of useful knowledge, I have seen many instances of young men who have been much hurt by what they expected to reap advantages from. They have gone to the academy humble, peaceable, spiritual, and lively; but have come out self-wise, dogmatical, censorious, and full of a prudence founded upon the false maxims of the world.' Newton does not necessarily blame theological colleges for such a lamentable change in students, but simply says that many theological students are themselves to be blamed, as students often gather ideas without seasoning them with grace and without balancing such ideas 'by a proportionable depth of spiritual experience'.

Among other advice given to the theological student, Newton counsels him not to concern himself with what belongs to the work of man and what belongs to the work of the Spirit when doing any study for sermons, as we ought to attribute everything to the work of the Spirit, since the means or methods employed to gain knowledge are God-ordained. The student ought not to hesitate in being diligent, except such diligence should be spiritual.

And what are the main ways by which a man becomes wise and thus suitable for the Christian ministry? Through the Scriptures and prayer. The Scriptures are the river of living water and prayer is the bucket by which we draw the water.

The Case for Meditation

Where does meditation come in? Meditation is derived from both the Scriptures and prayer. In what way is it derived from them? Newton says: '[Meditation is] a disposition of mind to observe carefully what passes within us and around us, what we see, hear and feel, and to apply all for the illustration and confirmation of the written word to us.' To Newton, meditation is more than merely thinking on a certain subject at a certain time. *Meditation is a state of mind, an acquired habit of observing what is going on in our heart as well as our outward circumstances, and observing how the Scriptures throw light on what is going on in our heart as well as in our outward circumstances and how the Scriptures are proven to be true by such observation.* Newton sees meditation as the hard work that brings profit (Proverbs 14:23), the treasures that the one who is instructed in the kingdom of heaven can bring out (Matthew 13:52), as the things that are seen and heard through observation and gathered in usefulness (1 John 1:3). No preacher of the Gospel can afford to be without the means of the Scriptures, prayer and meditation. 'The wisest can do nothing without them, the weakest shall not use them in vain.'

Meditation is not confined to the study of the Word and prayer as it touches also on what is in our heart and the nature of our circumstances; for the minister of the Gospel there is also the need to reflect on what people say and do in order to bring home to the hearers an apt message.

In the words of Newton we are 'to study the living as well as the dead'. Get around experienced Christians, get to know the weak Christians, take note of the many states and levels of spirituality you find them all in, observe how their minds work, what they say, how they reason in their various states of mind. Think on how one can console and so on, and what kind of answers one can anticipate will come each time, noticing how such things compare with the Word of God and what is in your own heart. Then 'what you observe of ten persons in these different situations, may be applied to ten thousand'. Circumstances may vary, but men universally all face the same problems. So preaching by reflecting on what the congregation is experiencing will bring home the truth of God. 'The converse I have with my people, usually suggests what I am to preach to them.'

In another of Newton's forty-one letters on religious subjects, there are three interesting letters addressed to the theme of the three different and advancing stages a Christian experiences in his life. These are pictured in terms of the growth of corn: first there is the blade, then the ear of corn, followed by the corn in full. Newton says the first stage of Christian experience is characterized by *desire*, when faith is weak but the heart is warm. The second stage has to do with *conflict*, when the believer, after thinking everything will be all right to the end for him, feels a change taking place inside him and learns 'the most sensible and distressing experience' of his evil nature. The third stage is marked by *contemplation*.

Naturally Newton does not mean that prior to stage three the believer has never done much thinking. The believer has been compelled to learn to think from hard experience – which experience compels him to think much about the nature of his heart and the need to trust the Lord. The heat of high emotion is no longer his, but in its place by the third stage is a judgement that is more solid, a mind that is more fixed, and 'thoughts more habitually exercised upon the things within the veil .... His contemplations are not barren speculations, but have a real influence, and enable him to exemplify the Christian character to more advantage, and with more consistence, than they can in the present state of things be expected either [from the first or the second stage of the Christian life].'

Contemplation and reflection appears in three ways in the seasoned believer: through humility, spirituality and through the union of heart to the glory and will of God. In humility the seasoned believer looks back on past perversity and his return to God, 'and how he has in a thousand instances rendered to the Lord evil for good'. The most experienced child of God 'knows most of himself, so he has seen most of the Lord'. This humility reaches out in the most mature way towards his fellow-believers as well. Such a humility has arisen through the Lord teaching us through the unexpected turns of life how much of the world is really in our hearts. This leads to a spirituality that only the seasoned believer knows, leads to seeing 'nothing [is] worth a serious thought, but communion with God and progress in holiness'.

Seeing that time is short, living on the foretaste of future glory, the Christian, who is the plant in full corn, has moved away (to change the metaphor) from being simply occupied with himself and his own comforts to being concerned with the glory of God, whether in life or in death. Upon the principle of seeking God's glory and will, his prayers, schemes and actions are formed.

In Letter XV of his forty-one letters on religious subjects, Newton, taking some liberty with the use of the term *book*, suggests to his reader there are four books one needs for a good Christian library. Of course, the first book needed is the Bible. The second and third books are the books of Creation and Providence. The fourth book? The book of the Heart, or Human Nature. The book Newton describes as 'comprehending the experiences of what passes within our own breasts, and the observations we make upon the principles and conduct of others, compared with what we read in the Word of God'.

The former slave-trader believed the heart is deep, but claimed the Scriptures are aware of this – the Scriptures make plain all the principles and the working of the human heart, in all possible circumstances, and all the ways by which the heart is affected by Satan, by sin, by things of the world, by grace, by solitude or company, in prosperity or affliction. Anything we observe in ourselves or in others will always be confirmed by God's Word. In a pregnant statement Newton writes what could be a wall text in many a place: 'Many, who are proud of their knowledge of what they might be safely ignorant of, are utter strangers to themselves.'

In this modern world, where we are bombarded with so much information that we can live without, many of us are strangers to ourselves. *We are told in these times not to be introspective because it is dangerous and it leads to an inferiority complex, but as Christians, who still have sin within us, we ought to become more acquainted with the evil which ever threatens to reign in our mortal bodies.* Lamentably the failure of not being acquainted with ourselves can be traced back to the same reason Newton puts forward when he says: 'Having no acquaintance with the Scripture, they have neither skill nor inclination to look into their own hearts, nor any certain criterion whereby to judge of the conduct of human life.'

We shall court danger if we look at ourselves with no other reference point, but, as John Newton reminds us, the Bible teaches us to read 'this mysterious book' of the human heart. The Scriptures uniquely show us the source, nature and tendency of our hopes, fears, desires, pursuits and perplexities. The Scriptures paint the reason why we are unhappy. The Scriptures display the uselessness and insufficiency of everything around us to help us. The Gospel exactly suits the desires and the wants of the awakened heart.

In *Cardiphonia* Newton writes twenty-six of the letters to a certain nobleman. In the fourth letter Newton expounds on the words of Galatians 5:17, where Paul writes, 'Ye cannot do the things ye would'. Newton suggests Christians have great desires given to them by the Lord, but they soon learn they cannot do what they wish to do, noble though their desires are. He claims he could make a long list of things believers would do if they could, but he restricts himself to four abilities (or four inabilities, whichever way one looks at them), one of which is the ability to have 'abiding, admiring thoughts of the person and love of the Lord Jesus Christ'.

Meditation is a difficult work. How often the Christian is ungrateful and insensible towards his best Friend and Benefactor. This reveals itself at the ease by which trivial thoughts arise and displace thoughts about Him who is the Beloved of our soul, who loved us and gave Himself for us, and whom we have chosen, deliberately chosen, as our chief good and portion. 'What can make amends for the loss we suffer here? Yet surely if we could, we would set Him always before us; His love should be the delightful theme of our hearts.'

Still, the former slave-trader does not leave us dwelling in despair. Although we cannot do the things we wish, even 'the distressing effects of the remnants of indwelling sin are over-ruled for good', as we are not under the law but under grace. By these distressing effects we are weaned off self and taught to cherish the need to rely on God. 'The more vile we are in our own eyes, the more precious He will be to us.' Our vileness has us longing for death, longing for the realm where the deep-rooted depravity will be in us no longer and at last we shall be able 'to do the thing we would'.

Newton felt that while some ministers of the Gospel can state and defend the Gospel well, while some have a talent for explaining difficult passages of Scripture, while some can ex-plain prophetic parts of the Word, and so on, he figured that anatomy was his favourite branch – and by this he meant the study of the human heart. Newton gave his mind to contemplate on all things related to the truth of God, but he spent considerable time contemplating on human behaviour in the light of the Gospel. He tells us in Letter XIII to a Nobleman that for a certain six weeks he spent several hours every day with sick and dying people. As he moved among them, he studied the heart 'with its workings and counter-workings,' as it acted and reacted in both nature and grace, as it responded to the differing conditions of prosperity, adversity, conviction, temptation, sickness and the approach of death. He felt he was fortunate to be observing poor people, who were not as pretentious as others and who had a certain simplicity in what they said and did, thus making Newton's observation easier.

He knew how fragile we are in the mind, and for this reason Newton believed we ought to be constantly in prayer for one another. Imagination is a wonderful power, yet 'it partakes largely of that depravity which sin has brought upon our whole frame, and affords Satan an avenue for assaulting us with the most terrifying, if not, the most dangerous of his temptations'. We cannot by willpower exclude many hurtful and painful ideas which are ever ready to obtrude on our minds, and it only takes a slight tilt in our emotions, our nervous system, to leave us wide open to the enemy of our souls. We can be shaken at the foundations so easily that we can become a terror to ourselves in those frightful times. 'All the Lord's people are not called on to navigate in these deep waters of soul distress; but all are liable.' For this reason we should pray for one another.

Judging on how liable we can be through the malice of our spiritual enemy, sensing our own weakness and knowing how ferocious the attacks can be, we should be able to sense what may happen to others and thus pray. 'Ah! if we knew what some suffer ... surely we would be more earnest and frequent in praying.'

Our ways with the world also have a bearing on the power of contemplating on holy things. John Newton supplies excellent advice in Letter XXV to a nobleman on how to move through the world as a believer. He says the world will leave us alone providing we acquiesce to their general customs and amusements, yet the world will wonder what is wrong with our religion if they find that we are seeking its company often – as if we do not have enough joy and comfort in the ways of God.

How should we conduct ourselves in the world? Let us mix with others as we must for our livelihood, but let us do our business with the world as one does business in the rain. Business calls us when it rains and we carry it out, though we may get wet, but once the business is done we get out of the rain. Duty calls us to be in the world and it will not hurt us if we find the spirit of the world unpleasant and we are glad to retire from it 'and keep out of it as much as our relative duties permit'.

The redeeming of our time is to be considered at this point. 'Much of it has already been lost, and therefore we are exhorted to redeem it.' We shall preclude much of what is customary in the world as being unsuitable for a believer, simply because we are meant to redeem the time. Do we need relaxation? Yes, of a kind. As long as 'the heart be alive,' relaxing will be rewarding. Can we live well a life divided between God and the world? Newton finds the solution in spending one part of our life in 'seeking after and conversing with Him whom our souls love,' and the other part employed in active service for the good of our family, friends, the church, and society for the Lord's sake. 'Every hour which does not fall in with one or other of these views, I apprehend is lost time.'

Still as part of *Cardiphonia*, we move on to one of two letters John Newton wrote to a Miss F——, in answer to the young lady's enquiry about the best way to prevent the world from drawing the heart away from God.

At the beginning he says we turn away from God rarely through ignorance of the proper means and motives by which we come to Him but rather from an evil principle within. He humbly offers his opinion as to how to reduce certain things to practice. It is our duty to walk closely to the Lord, but we must not expect perfection. Harrowing experiences will teach us not to expect perfection. Through experience we grow to become like a little child, who is afraid of taking a step alone, without God's help.

Three means ought to be employed to step out with God. The first is prayer. The second is attention to the Scriptures. The third is consideration or recollection, paying 'a careful regard to those temptations and snares, to which, from our tempers, situations or connections, we are more immediately exposed, and by which we have been formerly hindered'.

Newton suggests early in the morning before we leave 'our chambers', it would be profitable to forecast what circumstances we think we will meet, but he fears lest such a practice becomes a mere form. He hopes essentially that Miss F—— will look to the Lord most of all as her guard and teacher, for no one teaches like He does.

Yes, John Newton gave himself to an unending study of the heart. Through both observation of people and reading of the Scriptures he grew very learned in this area. For him there was no end to such a study, whether the subject was related to his own heart or the hearts of others. With reference to his own heart, he confessed that after twenty-eight years since the Lord began to open his own heart for himself to see, almost every day there was discovered by him something that previously was unobserved. Moreover, as the days progressed the more Newton believed that he had observed only a little of what was in his own heart. He likened it all to some parts of Derbyshire, England, where the country is cavernous, but superficial observation does not reveal how large and deep and numerous the caverns are.

He contended that young believers, soon after they are converted, ought to begin studying the ways of their own hearts. Too many young believers are caught out by pride and presumption, thinking themselves full of grace when they mistake the early zeal for true righteousness. Only a study of one's own heart can make one receptive and fruitful in righteousness, for the eradication of evil dispositions and practices is necessary for any growth in holiness. Many a young believer would spare himself or herself much pain if he or she took to aiding the process of sanctification and conforming to the ways of God fully by looking closely at what is in the heart. It requires time to go through all the rooms, one after another, in the heart, and the sooner the believer begins, the more prosperous he or she will be.

What Newton applies to unbelievers in his sermon *On the Deceitfulness of the Heart* (Jeremiah 17:9,10) can well be applied to believers too. What if every thought that has ever passed our minds were declared openly in public, if every thought and every wish was broadcast openly? Newton ventures to say that many would rather die than comply with that kind of ordeal. He says the Lord has mercifully kept us from the knowledge of each other's hearts, by keeping us from knowing no more than what people are willing to disclose of themselves.

While he holds the believer is wonderfully delivered from condemnation once he trusts in Christ, the former slave-trader still contends the believer's soul is like a besieged city, with enemies outside the gates longing to get in, and restless traitors inside the city eager to betray and who regularly secretly correspond with the enemies outside in planning our downfall.

In the light of this how can any child of God fail to reflect on what is happening, what could happen and what should happen by the grace of God?

There is no time for anyone at all to lose in such contemplation either. Newton advises a young fellow who is waiting to enter the ministry to use up the in-between time he has for the benefit of the future. He tells the young fellow that he will become more acquainted with the Gospel, also with his own heart and with human nature, if he takes to being content 'with being a learner in the school of Christ for some years'. He is particularly told to study human nature as it 'is a necessary branch of a minister's knowledge, and can only be acquired by comparing what passes within us, and around us, with what we read in the Word of God'.

In these days when there is much accent on the love and the grace of God, when we have shied away from what we think is the dreadful edge of morbid introspection, there is a need to take Newton's counsel seriously. The danger with the accent on the love and grace of God lies in the fact that such an accent, while seeming to bathe in the light of truth, is in the lengthening shadows of half-truth. No one will decry the need to preach and teach the love, grace and all-sufficiency of God, for our greatest need is to be aware of such truth, but we have gone beyond the pale of Scripture when we refuse to look inwardly and only look outwardly.

We all love to hear of God's grace, forgiveness of sin, God's free love, and so on, but, unless we believers search the heart with a mind to uprooting the residual sin in it, we will never come to a true knowledge of grace itself. *We may be very knowledgeable in the head when it comes to the truth of divine grace, but we may not be all that skilled in searching the soil in our hearts where grace can only truly thrive when the obnoxious weeds are pulled out.* It is a harder work to uproot the weeds and prepare the soil than to plant the flowers of grace, and perhaps laziness as well as ignorance has led many to go the easy way and think more or less only in terms of divine grace.

If we neglect the work of self-examination, we shall be easy prey for self-deceit. We will think we are objects, dear objects of God's grace, when sin is actually preventing us from genuine and lasting fellowship with God. We will be quick to blame God should anything too adverse happen to us, not understanding that the Divine Surgeon, kind as He is, is anxious to cure us of ills in the soul. We will be slow to recognize the glory and greatness of God, even though we thought we understood His grace. As believers, the sooner we learn of God's greatness, glory, holiness, power, majesty and authority as well, as our own sinful and abject condition (yes, even as believers), the better.

We may complain that talk of self-examination with a view

to seeing our residual sinfulness as a believer has too much to do with a strictness that the Gospel of pardoning sin will not own, yet many modern Christians are defeated Christians. Why? One reason lies in them actually abusing God's grace when they think they are availing themselves of it with His glad consent. When we do not consider how putrefying sin is in the eyes of God, and we have not endeavoured to search it out and uproot it from our hearts, we will have false hopes and not realise God may not be in communion with us at all, because we have cheapened His grace. Grace is undeserved help. Let us respect it for what it is.

We also have the habit of preaching and teaching in *general* in the Western church today. We do not wish to appear legalistic, so we shy away from particularizing about sin. For example, who hears anything said about gluttony in these times? We are resting in the general aim of doing things for the glory of God, rather like a man who is going on a journey and takes no notice of the particular turns he has to make – obviously, he does not reach the end of the journey.

John Owen reminds us in his *Indwelling Sin in Believers* that John wrote 1 John with an order and method of doctrine we would do well to obey: 'This is the order and method of the doctrine of the Gospel, and of the application of it to our soul : first to keep us from sin and *then* to relieve against sin.' Today there is much talk about relief from sin, and little, if any, about the Gospel keeping us from sin. John Owen of the seventeenth century lamented that the church often takes up the last theme of John's letter – the theme of forgiveness – and makes it the first, and excludes the first theme! We would do well to remember Owen's counsel when he says the Gospel proposes there is pardon for sin, but it principally proposes the keeping of ourselves from sin.

Now we see why so few believers of today find little need of

meditation in the way John Newton of the eighteenth century did.
If we think living by the Gospel only requires some passing
recognition of God's grace and free love, especially with a view
to being forgiven of our sins, then, to put it perhaps somewhat
crudely, there is not much to think about.

On the other hand, if we understand living by the Gospel to
mean searching our hearts closely and strictly each day to root
out any evil, lest we lose the joy and peace of God's grace, crying
out for His grace because we have not learnt as we ought the
painful truth that sin resides within us no matter how we wish to
be rid of it, then meditation will be employed in the struggle.

The craftier and the stronger the enemy appears, the more we
have to think of strategies to overcome him. To a large measure
the strategies are in the Word of God, but they are strategies that
need to be employed ever against a deceiving, treacherous and
relentless sinfulness in the believer's heart.

Of course, Newton did not leave us lying in the slough of
introspection. Just as the believer finds the heart's rooms, one
after the other, full of evil potential and beyond comprehension,
so he finds as more than a mere counterbalance the incomprehensible love of Jesus, a love that no exploration can ever discover
its limits. The love of Jesus ought to be a constant theme of our
thoughts, for, after all, though we are sanctified sinners, we are
sanctified and destined to be taken one day to be with Him who
is perfect love, living with Him with a heart that needs no longer
to be searched for any hidden sin.

9

MARTYN LLOYD-JONES

Martyn Lloyd-Jones is particularly remembered for his thirty years as the preacher and pastor of Westminster Chapel in London. He died in 1981 and has been described by many as the greatest preacher the English-speaking world has seen this century.

He was born in rural Wales in 1899. He grew up in church life when worship was entertainment and when it was often presumed that everyone who passed through the church doors was a Christian. At the age of 23 he became Chief Clinical Assistant to Sir Thomas Horder, the King's doctor, but in his twenties his soul was troubled by the thought of sin while under John Hutton's preaching in London. When he spent a number of weeks reclassifying his chief's case histories according to their respective illnesses and diseases, Lloyd-Jones discovered that perhaps as many as 70 per cent could not be classified as having any particular medical disorder. Therefore, Lloyd-Jones grew in a conviction that he could serve God better by putting behind a promising and illustrious career as a doctor and preaching the Gospel. This he did when at 27 he went to pastor a struggling Calvinistic Methodist Mission Church in Abernavon, South Wales, where he had a remarkable ministry. In one year alone the church saw an addition of 135 to the membership, of whom 128 were 'from the world'.

On the eve of World War II he went to London, where he became minister of Westminster Chapel. At first he faced a daunting struggle, both in the war years and the immediate postwar years, but his hard work paid off in the fifties and sixties, when Lloyd-Jones exerted an enormous influence on the whole evangelical world as well as on the Chapel.

Often alone in combating the insipidness of the Christian churches in the fifties and sixties, he proved that loyalty to the Scriptures and power of the Spirit makes for a more abiding and fruitful ministry than the provision of entertainment. People from all walks of life flocked to the Chapel to hear an earnest man engage in the simplicity of preaching. His presence in the pulpit was awesome. Someone described the Welshman's power in these terms: 'At times, often towards the end of the sermon, he seemed to be hovering, waiting for something. Sometimes the wind of the Spirit would come and sweep us and him aloft, and we would mount with wings as eagles into the awesome and felt presence of God. Under his preaching big, grown men would cry.'

He decried the idea that people could believe in Christ without emotion, but his preaching was always tempered by the objectivity of truth. He fervently believed that Christian doctrine was not being given the pre-eminence it ought to occupy in the minds of people. He thought too many people think too much about themselves. Once he told a woman who came to see him for counselling because she was depressed and confused: 'Refuse to think about yourself.' *This says much about Martyn Lloyd-Jones, whose burning drive was to take men off themselves and become preoccupied with the sovereign greatness of God in Christ.*

He enlisted his short experience as a doctor of medicine to become a doctor of souls. He was interested in psychology, but believed modern psychology fails because it teaches people how to look within and how to analyse one's mind and motives, assuming that the primary need is to possess a knowledge of oneself. Lloyd-Jones firmly believed the starting point has to be a knowledge of God. Much that passes as a psychological problem is essentially spiritual. Spiritual understanding is the crying need. He claimed that in his thirty-four years of pastoral experience, people most frequently got into trouble in their spiritual experience because they lacked understanding of the Scriptures.

Lloyd-Jones preached in such a way that he counselled many people all at the same time, so that more than one person who had planned to see him in the vestry after the worship service, felt there was no longer any need to do so. He lamented the modern approach of preachers (so-called), who preach little because they believe more time ought to be spent on counselling and interviewing. Lloyd-Jones did a little counselling on the side in his unique way, but he believed 'preaching is the highest and the greatest and the most glorious calling to which anyone can ever be called' and through it much of the counsel is done.

His manysidedness is exemplified in a certain book that formed a tribute to him after he died. In the book contributions are made by a considerable number of renowned people, and Lloyd-Jones' ministry is viewed from the standpoint of his place: in evangelicalism as a whole, as a doctor, as a preacher, as a leader among evangelical students, as a theologian, a family man, as a pastor's pastor, as an encourager, a friend, and as a man who influenced many throughout the world.

It must be said Lloyd-Jones saw himself primarily as an evangelist. Certainly his preaching led to countless people being saved over the years, even though he did not employ the decision system that is rife today among evangelists; in addition no statistics were used to keep a record of the numbers of those who turned to Christ under his ministry. Lloyd-Jones' wife often corrected people who looked on her husband as a teacher rather than an evangelist. More than half of his preaching was directed at unbelievers.

All the same, he contributed much to the notion of Christian meditation because he championed the need to be acquainted with doctrine when evangelicalism was seeing Christian experience only in terms of the subjectivity of one's emotions and feelings or in the one-sided practicality of Christian works. For a man who advocated the purest of motive for all that we think, feel and do, contemplation of an analytical but spiritual kind was viewed as most essential.

Right from the beginning of the first of his 260 or so sermons in his series on Ephesians[1], which series he began on October 10, 1954, Dr Lloyd-Jones made it clear the Bible is God's book, *and our thinking must start with God.* He said:

> Much of the trouble in the Church today is due to the fact that we are so subjective, so interested in ourselves, so egocentric. Having forgotten God, and having become so interested in ourselves, we become miserable and wretched, and spend our time in 'shallows and miseries'. We must not start by examining ourselves and our needs microscopically; we must start with God, and forget ourselves. We must not begin with ourselves and ascend to God; we must start with the sovereignty of God, God over all, and then come down to ourselves.[2]

He would go on to say in the fourth sermon of Ephesians that it is not a lack of superficial knowledge of the Scriptures today, but a lack of knowledge of the doctrines of the Scriptures. As God's

---

1. The Banner of Truth Trust, Edinburgh, Scotland have published the sermons in a series of eight volumes: *God's Ultimate Purpose* (1:1-23); *God's Way of Reconciliation* (2:1-22); *Unsearchable Riches of Christ* (3:1-21); *Christian Unity* (4:1-16); *Darkness and Light* (4:17-5:17); *Life in the Spirit* (5:18-6:9); *Christian Warfare* (6:10-13); *Christian Soldier* (6:10-20).
2. *God's Ultimate Purpose*, page 13.

people, we do not know who we are, what we are, and why we are what we are. For him every verse of Ephesians had to be treated 'very carefully'. Of course, Christianity is about experience and the experimental, but 'indeed, it is the extent of our understanding that ultimately determines our experience'. Our problem often lies in taking one chapter at a time when reading God's word, and we never stop to analyse and realise what it is saying to us. Some excuse themselves by claiming they are 'practical' Christians, but the Scriptures have been written so we may understand spiritual truths.

Lloyd-Jones shows the logic of Paul in Ephesians, the kind of logic we ought to adopt to derive blessing from the Father. In Sermon Seven he talks of 'spiritual blessings in high places', and says Ephesians 1:3 talks about them in a general manner. He claims Paul anticipates such questions as 'How does any Christian ever enjoy a single blessing?' and that Paul proceeds to amplify his general statement. From verse 4 to verse 14 we have a description of the blessings. Although in regard to the doctrine of the sovereignty of God in salvation, some believers do not hold it, Lloyd-Jones shows it is not necessary for us to believe it to be saved. Then it does not matter? Oh, no! – 'my understanding of it does not determine my salvation, (yet) it does determine my experience of the joy of salvation, and the sense of security and certainty'. As believers we may not bow the knee to all of Scripture's logic, but in regard to the blessing promised we will be the losers.

In Lloyd-Jones' mind Scripture is written in the way it is because it is word-for-word the Word of God. Sometimes we meet with a chronological arrangement for its words, sometimes we meet with a logical one.

The Apostle Paul, for one, varies his terms, but not to rescue his writing from the monotonous – no, he varies them to bring a certain force and intensity related to the subject. Says Lloyd-Jones in regard to a certain variation of terms: 'As we come to consider this, let us remind ourselves that when we are reading the Scriptures we must never take anything for granted. We must always be alert and alive, and always ready to ask questions. How easily one can miss the great blessings found in the very introduction of an Epistle such as this by simply sliding over the terms as if they did not matter!'

He likens looking at the Scriptures to looking at pictures in an art gallery, only we must not be like those who pass quickly through and say they have 'done' the gallery. 'It is surely better to stand, if necessary, for hours before this chapter (Ephesians 1), which has been given to us by God Himself through His Spirit, and to gaze upon it, and to try to discover its riches both in general and in detail.'

Lloyd-Jones says poignantly in Sermon 28 of Ephesians: 'The best way of profiting from reading the Scriptures is to ask questions of the Scriptures, to talk to the Scriptures, to take every phrase carefully and ask, "Why did he say this, why that?" '[3]

Combating Spiritual Depression

The great preacher of Westminster Chapel tackles spiritual depression quite differently from the way many Christian counsellors of modern times do. In his book *Spiritual Depression – Its Causes and Its Cure,* he surprises with his doctrinal approach, spiced only now and then with stories and illustrations. Lloyd-Jones believed too many attempt to feed off other people's experiences or covet them, instead of looking away to 'this great doctrinal teaching, plain and clear,' which God in His grace has given to us. Lloyd-Jones only adds illustrations in the book when it is necessary to bring out 'the great principles being worked out

3. *God's Ultimate Purpose*, page 329.

in practice'. While it is true that Lloyd-Jones, towards the end of his life, lamented that he did not use enough illustrations in his sermons throughout his preaching career, one need not believe he would have contemplated retracting from the doctrinal approach he adopted for principles in *Spiritual Depression*. More illustrations, yes, but never to the detriment of obscuring the primary and most fundamental principles of the Christian faith.

In dealing with depression, he firstly ensures that people examine themselves to see if in fact they are believers first of all. Some depressed people have had a religious or Christian background, but they do not know what it is to be justified. They see the Gospel in terms of being sanctified, instead of asking themselves if they are justified and accepted by God in the first place. They may be content with vague religion – and vague religion is easy to live with on appearances and consequently popular – and are apt to mix their own ideas with spiritual truth.

They want nothing to do with doctrine, as 'It is the doctrine that hurts, it is the doctrine that focuses things'. Lloyd-Jones likens such people to the man who was partly cured by Jesus of blindness and 'saw men as trees walking' – they think they see, but ought not to testify when they cannot see clearly. Lloyd-Jones somewhat inconsistently has the man of Mark 8 being presumptuous by claiming he can see when he partly sees only, and at the same time counts the man as being honest for testifying he can only partly see. But all the same the point is taken: Do we really see the things of salvation as the Bible suggests we should, and are we being honest by acknowledging we are blind until we see?

As for believers, their spiritual depression may well begin because of the circumstances accompanying their conversion, that is, their conversion came about through circumstances where the whole Gospel was not the centre of attention. Some

believers are born again thinking the Gospel is only about mere
forgiveness. Such incomplete views Lloyd-Jones pits against
'the form of doctrine', 'the standard of teaching' such as Paul
elaborates in his letter to the Romans 'with its mighty arguments
and propositions and its flight of spiritual imagination'. Incomplete and partial views of the Gospel deprive many believers of
the happiness they ought to possess. Such incomplete and partial
views may also arise because some emphasize the head too
much, some the heart, some the will. One must remember *how*
one has become a Christian. It must be understood that the truth
is presented to the *mind*. Then having seen the truth, *the heart*
is moved to accept it. Then the will is exercised in the desiring
of it. 'The heart is always to be influenced through the understanding - the mind, then the heart, then the will.'

Once a person believes in Christ, there comes to him 'that one
sin' which dogs many a believer and causes deep depression - sin
to do with the past, 'some particular sin of their past', or ...'the
particular form which sin happens to take in their case'. The
surprising thing is that Lloyd-Jones suggests such people ought
not to pray! Such people often and only pray, and their problem
is not solved. Why not pray? Because prayer only reminds one
of the problem. Then what should such a believer do? He should
stop praying and *think*. Think about what? Think about doctrine.

Let Lloyd-Jones speak for himself:

> That is the great New Testament doctrine on this matter; it is the
> thing that these people have to grasp above everything else, that
> we must not think in terms of particular sins but always in terms
> of our relationship to God. We all tend to go astray at that point.
> That is why we tend to think some conversions are more
> remarkable than others. But they are not. It takes the same grace
> of God to save the most respectable person in the world as the
> most lawless person in the world. Nothing but the grace of God

can save anybody, and it takes the same grace to save all. But we do not think like that. We think some conversions are more remarkable than others. *Because we are wrong in our doctrine* (italics mine), we differentiate between sin and sin, and think some sins are worse than others. It all comes back to our relationship to God; it is all a matter of belief or unbelief.[4]

Lloyd-Jones has us constantly coming back to *thinking,* and *thinking on doctrine as it is spelt out in the Scriptures.* When writing of Christians who are timid and fear the future, he states: 'Our fears are due to our failure to stir up – failure to think, failure to take ourselves in hand.' Our imagination may run away with us. It could be said imagination is thinking of a kind, and some may conclude that therefore it is best to think less. Yet Lloyd-Jones defines 'thinking' that overcomes fear in terms of taking a firm grip on ourselves, pulling ourselves up, stirring up ourselves, taking ourselves in hand and speaking to ourselves. He says graphically, 'In other words, we have to learn to say, that what matters in any of these positions is not what is true of us but what is true of Him.'

It is tempting to believe that the great preacher of Westminster Chapel could afford to write this way as he probably had a choleric temperament with the natural inclination to collect himself, get up and get going. Yet the reader, if he had been tempted to dismiss the man's advice because of this, is suddenly confronted by the fact Lloyd-Jones is aware of temperamental differences amongst men.

All the same, difference of temperament cannot lend an excuse to failing to overcome fear. As Christians we ought never to be controlled by our temperaments. The Holy Spirit ought to control us, control our temperament. We notice he does not say the Holy Spirit crushes our temperament. No, regeneration does

4. *Spiritual Depression*, published by Marshall Pickering, page 71.

not dispense with it. We still possess it, but the Holy Spirit enables us in our own particular way to function with our temperament. When the Spirit takes control, we forget self and become absorbed in the things of God.

With respect to temperaments, Lloyd-Jones makes an interesting reference to the apostle Peter in the eleventh chapter of *Spiritual Depression*.[5] I am not certain if Dr Martin Lloyd-Jones subscribed to the traditional view of the four temperaments of man (sanguine, choleric, melancholic and phlegmatic), but his description of Peter fits in with the traditional view so that Peter is depicted as sanguine and given to acting without thinking on many occasions.

Lloyd-Jones describes Peter as having the temperament that leads to impulsiveness and impetuosity. In the Gospels he is always the first to volunteer, and Lloyd-Jones cites the incident of the disciples fishing all night and Peter is the first to jump into the water when John recognized it was Jesus on the shore. Even after Pentecost he was still on some occasions the unthinking man.

Was his temperament to blame? Lloyd-Jones does not excuse him. He says Peter's trouble was his faith was not based on sufficient thought. He did not work things out. For instance, he knew of the doctrine of justification but he failed to work out its implications, consequently at Antioch Paul exposed his hypocrisy. He had no excuse, thinking intuitively rather than understanding and grasping the truth thoroughly. This, says Lloyd-Jones, is what passes as spiritual depression among many of God's children. *When meditation ought to rest on the true things of God, instead it is resting on things of the world, which things are beyond our depth, just as Peter was out of his depth when attempting to cross the water to meet Jesus.*

---

5. *Spiritual Depression*, published by Marshall Pickering.

Doubts are not incompatible with faith, but we must not let doubts master us. Peter leant on 'feeling' in his attempt to cross the water, but feeling has no value unless it is based on a sound knowledge of Jesus Christ. 'In other words, the great antidote to spiritual depression is the knowledge of Biblical doctrine, Christian doctrine.'

The Case for Sound Teaching

In knowing the preacher of Westminster Chapel believed depression is largely cured by a knowledge of true doctrine, it need not surprise us to come across a chapter solely on false teaching. I know of no other modern book on spiritual depression and doubts and anxiety that deals with false teaching as a cause of such, but Dr Lloyd-Jones was of a different mould from that found in our present times, not viewing the cause of depression and inferiority as stemming from the lack of psychological self-esteem. In the fifties and sixties, when Lloyd-Jones was pastor of Westminster Chapel, cross-pollination of the Gospel with modern, secular psychology – with its emphasis on self-esteem – was already apparent, but the great preacher, while cognizant of the attempt to cross-pollinate, remained unmoved in his conviction that the Word of God contains all the counsel any believer needs. Believers seek out psychological clinics not because the Word has nothing to say about their predicaments, but because they are ignorant of what it does say. Lloyd-Jones was no theorist; time and again he saw his conviction confirmed when men and women under his preaching of the Word found counsel and help without having to resort to a psychologist or psychiatrist.

In 1977 Lloyd-Jones contrasted Paul's method of helping Christians and the modern approach of counselling. He believed that 'much that passes among Christians now as psychological problems is essentially spiritual'. He wrote in *Preaching and Preachers*: 'My experience is that most of the people who come to ask for the name of a Christian psychiatrist need spiritual help rather than psychiatric treatment.'[6] For him psychology teaches a man how to look within and how to analyse one's mind and motives. The object is to know one's self.

According to Scripture, the object ought to be to know God. He could say after being a pastor for thirty-four years, up to 1961, that the people he found most frequently in trouble in their spiritual experience had been those who had lacked understanding. Most of our troubles are due to starting with man and ending with man. At times he came across cases that he classified 'psychological', and cases where people had mental or physical difficulties, but in most cases, after discerning whether or not the one seeking help was an actual believer, he viewed the problem as having spiritual causes. He was fond of reminding Christians that their need was not the 'hospital' but the 'barracks', thus forgetting their own ills and learning to fight in the army.

It is with the 'barracks' concept in mind that we ought to view the chapter 'False Teaching' in Lloyd-Jones' book *Spiritual Depression*. False teachers infiltrate the ranks of believers, just as they did in the days Paul wrote his letter of combat to the Galatians. Quoting Galatians 4:15, 'Where is then the blessedness ye spake of?' Lloyd-Jones points out the Galatian Christians were unhappy. Now, why were they unhappy?

Paul rightly attributes it to false teaching, the false teaching that was not so much a denial of the faith as a teaching which suggested something else is required in addition to what is already believed. The glory of Lloyd-Jones' teaching, as it has already been stated, lay in his conviction the Bible is 'the most up-to-date Book,' and he proceeds in *False Teaching* to show

6. Published by Hodder and Stoughton, London.

that the Galatian heresy has its modern counterparts, so that believers even today, after having experienced the joy of amazing blessing of knowing God in Christ, are introduced to another kind of teaching that seems so spiritual and 'promises such unusual blessing if they believe it'. When they adopt the new teaching, they become confused, perplexed and most miserable, losing their first happiness.

Thinking Spiritually
Such deluded believers must get around to right thinking. They must test themselves by the authoritative teaching of Scripture, just as the Galatians were called on to see that the only standard for them was the apostolic message Paul and the apostles of Jerusalem preached. Testing ourselves by the authoritative message of Scripture includes the implications of such teaching as well. Even the apostle Peter once failed to see the implications. As Lloyd-Jones points out, Peter did not want to deny salvation through Christ by faith, and yet he was denying it through his hypocrisy, such hypocrisy that suggested something in addition to faith in Christ is necessary. All this is borne out in Galatians 2, where we have the record of Paul withstanding Peter to his face over the issue.

Lloyd-Jones goes on in the remainder of *False Teaching* to show what characterizes heresy and false teaching, clearly showing that he himself has thought through such things. At the beginning of his ministry at Westminster he stressed Christians must think aright about God. Thinking aright must even be put before prayer. *Christians should not simply gain comfort from passages of Scripture, but must think theologically about them, and be concerned with the details of Scripture with a disciplined mind.*

In 1953–54 Dr Lloyd-Jones preached eleven sermons on

Psalm 73 (these sermons came out in a book[7] called *Faith on Trial*), in which he saw as pivotal the importance of spiritual thinking. He takes note that the Psalmist, in wrestling with both the problem of the prosperity of the wicked and the troubles of the godly, gains a foothold first by realizing his hasty conclusions were wrong and that he must not say what he was tempted to say lest it causes the downfall of those of his generation. But he notes that such a foothold was only the beginning of climbing back to spiritual ascendancy. The Psalmist got the rebellious thoughts under control, but his thoughts were going around and around in circles, so that he was still in great anguish of heart. The reason for his thoughts going around and around in circles? The Psalmist was thinking rationally, not spiritually.

Let Lloyd-Jones show us the difference:

This is a tremendously important principle. It is very difficult to put into language the difference between purely rational thinking and spiritual thinking, because someone may be tempted to say, 'Ah yes, there it is again. I have always said Christian thinking is irrational.' But that is a false deduction. While I draw a distinction between rational thinking and spiritual thinking, I am not for a moment suggesting spiritual thinking is irrational. The difference between them is that rational thinking is ground level only; spiritual thinking is equally rational, but it takes in a higher level as well as a lower level. *It takes in all the facts instead of some of them* [italics mine]. ...There is a constant danger of slipping back to merely rational thinking even in our Christian life. This is a very subtle thing. Without realizing it at all, though we are Christians, though we are born again, though we have the Holy Spirit in us, there is a constant danger

---

7. *Faith Tried and Triumphant,* published by Baker Book House, Grand Rapids, USA in an edition uniting two books published earlier, *From Fear To Faith* and *Faith On Trial*.

of our reverting to a type of thinking that has nothing to do with Christianity at all. The Psalmist was a devout and godly man, one who had had great experience at the hand of God; but quite unconsciously he had reverted to that merely rational type of thinking. Perhaps I can put this point still more clearly by saying that we have to learn that the whole of the Christian life is spiritual and not merely parts of it. [8]

By 'the whole of the Christian life' he means our Christian life from the time of conversion to the end of our life. When we become Christians we are acutely aware of thinking on a new plane, on a higher as well as a lower plane, but mainly on a higher plane. We know as Christians that the trouble with those who are not Christians lies in their inability to think in no more than rational terms, but our trouble as Christians is that we frequently relapse into the way we used to think before we were converted, in the way we know the unconverted think. We may not be all that conscious of it, but we are constantly dropping back to the rational level of thinking. Any complaint or grudge we have bears testimony to it. Therefore, in the course of every stage, every phase, every interest, every development of our Christian life, we must learn to think spiritually. We need to ask ourselves: Am I facing this spiritually? Am I recollecting that this is a question of my relationship to God? Am I sure my thinking is spiritual at this point?

What constituted spiritual thinking for the Psalmist and what constitutes it for us? Lloyd-Jones takes us with the Psalmist to the sanctuary of God, to where the believers met.

In Lloyd-Jones' mind this starts the process of spiritual thinking for the Psalmist, who, in attending the sanctuary of God, realizes that while he has a terrible personal problem, the church

---

8. *Faith Tried and Triumphant*, page 101.

has existed for long years under the plan of God and the personal problem begins to pale among people who believe worship of God is most worthwhile. The Psalmist begins to say, according to Lloyd-Jones : 'Perhaps I may be wrong; all these people think there is something in it; they may be right.' As he looks around the sanctuary, he sees people with worse problems than he has, and he also reflects on the saints of the past, the saints who courageously by their faith overcame all kinds of adversities. The process of spiritual thinking continues through the reading of God's Word and through prayer.

Lloyd-Jones is careful, however, when he considers prayer as part of spiritual thinking. He makes short shrift of those who always say to fellow-believers, 'Pray about it,' as if it is the panacea of all problems. 'Pray about it' can be glib, superficial advice. It would have been so for the author of Psalm 73, whose thinking was too muddled in order for him to pray. 'Before we can pray truly we must think spiritually.' The physician-turned-preacher cites the practice of George Muller, who as many believers know, excelled in prayer. Muller for many years used to rush into prayer each morning, but then he discovered it was not the best way. Instead, he prepared himself, ensuring he was in the Spirit before prayer. 'Very often we waste our time thinking we are praying when we are not really praying at all.'

Therefore Lloyd-Jones concludes his sermon on 'The Importance of Spiritual Thinking': 'So the steps are perfectly right – the house of God, the Word of God and communion with God'.

Yet Lloyd-Jones does not end his references to right thinking at the end of 'The Importance of Spiritual Thinking'[9]. He goes on to show the author of Psalm 73 faced all the facts as well as reaching a proper understanding of spiritual truth. Is religion nothing but 'the opiate of the people'? Some in their unthinking

---

9. *op. cit.*, page 112

seek through worship a euphoric sense of happiness and well-being without their mind being employed. Are we more concerned about being happy or knowing the truth? Knowing the truth in facing all the facts and thinking things right through? The author of Psalm 73 put this thinking right in general, and then he put right certain particulars, such as the correct view of God and His character, His covenant promises and faithfulness, God's 'sleepiness' and the reasons for it, what happens when God 'wakes up'.

Furthermore, the author of Psalm 73 was put right in regard to himself, after being put right in regard to the ungodly and to God. He comes to repent of his foolish thoughts. How does he repent? 'This repentance, this state in which someone pauses and looks at himself and talks to himself about himself, is one of the most essential and vital aspects of what is commonly called the discipline of the Christian life.'

The Pitfalls of Self-examination

At this point Lloyd-Jones alerts us to two dangers involving self-examination: one to do with morbid introspection, the other to do with the tendency to spare ourselves and treat our sin too lightly. Of the two dangers the latter is easily our problem in modern times. In modern times 'we are much too glib, and much too superficial'. Now, what does repentance entail? It is not merely sliding over our sin as believers, it is looking at our sin 'in all its details and [considering] all that it involves and implies'. Although it is painful to do, like the Psalmist we ought to particularize about our sin. It is easier just to say 'I am sinful' than to name the sins of which we are actually guilty. The spiritual masters of every age have always named them. We ought to be indignant of ourselves. And when we become indignant in this way, we find that the cause of all our troubles is really 'self'. Lloyd-Jones puts it well:

> The Psalmist found out that that really was the cause of all his
> troubles. He had gone wrong in thinking about the ungodly, he had
> gone wrong in thinking about God. But the ultimate cause of all his
> troubles was that he had gone wrong in thinking about himself.[10]

In true psychology (biblical psychology), Lloyd-Jones asserts,
self is seen to take control because the heart always goes before
the head. The Psalmist thought he was being rational. 'Look at
them! Look at me!' He was being governed by his feelings. He
gave himself a hard time by looking at things wrongly. He was
like an animal, reacting to impulse, rather than being logical and
balanced. We are admonished to remember that whenever we
are beset with perplexities, we ought to view everything in terms
of God's purposes and the whole view of salvation. To do
anything less is stupid.

Lastly, the Psalmist had gone wrong in his view about the
godly and the godly life. He misinterpreted the role of trouble
in a believer's life. Like an animal, he resented discipline. He
was stupid, which led him to being ignorant. Yet he has confessed his foolishness and is on the way up to acknowledging
'God is good to Israel'. He had been foolish, but God has not
deserted him – no, he is still with God! God is gracious. He then
realizes the future is bright, assured that the Lord will lead him
to the end, even to glory. So he goes from almost making public
his despair to his fellow-believers, to the radical acknowledge-
ment that there is no one but God that he desires – desiring God
and desiring nothing but God.

He had mistaken the root cause of his trouble to be the
prosperity of the wicked and the troubles of the godly, but the
root cause lay in his failure to be near God. He virtually
concludes, 'If I am near God, it does not matter what happens to

---

10. *op. cit.,* page 149.

me'. All this wonderfully supports Lloyd-Jones' thesis: 'The Bible never gives us a general injunction; it always gives us reasons for it.' If this is so, then it is the studious, reflective believer who in persistence in meditation will arrive at a true understanding of God's Word and be able to keep his head when tested.

The Serious Preacher

In the late forties, when Dr Martyn Lloyd-Jones was building up his congregation at Westminster Chapel, after it had dwindled considerably on the heels of World War II, there were some memorable sermons he preached with much conviction and power. In those times he related to one of his daughters by letter:

> Several came to see me at the end. It was certainly a night of much conviction and I felt I was being used. But oh! how far short do we fall of Paul's description of the Christian. *If only we knew more about and meditated more upon the glory that awaits us...* [italics mine]

The fact that the great man was conscious of the need to meditate meant he did meditate, and did meditate on the glory to come. We do not know how he meditated, nor for how long – we know little about the way some of the great men of God did it – but it is difficult to imagine that a man such as Lloyd-Jones, who preached with unique power throughout the long period from the Twenties to the Sixties (both in Wales and England), could have preached with all the success he had unless he was given to serious and extended periods of deep contemplation on the things of God. Not just the length of years of preaching testifies to this, but the kind of preaching he engaged in.

Much of his preaching at Westminster was expository over three decades. He did a series on Philippians, a series on 1 John,

60 gripping sermons on Ephesians, from 1955 to 1968 he preached on Romans, in 1959 26 messages on revival to mark the centenary of the Irish Revival, a series on John's Gospel, a series on Acts, other series of a lesser nature, all this until March, 1968, when illness finished his ministry at Westminster just when he had reached his 372nd exposition on Romans.

In doing such series he was following the Puritan tradition, and arguably his expositions were on a par with the Puritans as far as fire and devotion were concerned, and certainly excelled the greater number of Puritans in terms of exegetical accuracy. He must have thought often and deeply, and not merely read other's opinions. His sermons reveal original thought, and went beyond the practice that some of his young admirers had adopted during the Fifties of simply living to read without the balance of spiritual depth and power. He always insisted that men ought to read but not to regurgitate what others have said – one can legitimately read others' thoughts, but there is the need to reflect on those thoughts until you work out that which becomes your own. Certainly the Welshman put such a thing into practice, so that while he was well-acquainted in admiration with the Puritans, Jonathan Edwards and others, his expository sermons were not echoes from another century. The truths, even the ones he learnt from others, became his own when out of deep thought and rich experience he reshaped them to make them more his own.

Serious Meditation
When illness overtook him in 1968, he began to know of the coming glory in a new way, for there was a sense of foreboding about the Inevitable. At a ministers' fraternal in late 1968 he solemnly spoke to his confreres about the folly of waiting for illness to happen to us before we give it thought, rather we should always be preparing for such a time. He admitted that we get

carried away by our routine until we are 'suddenly pulled up'. He quoted Edmund Burke, who remarked on the death of a political opponent: 'What shadows we are, what shadows we pursue.' He went on to say: 'We tend to exaggerate things which in the end are not vital, allowing ourselves to be moved over-much. In the light of eternity we see things at their real value.'

In the Seventies, as the sales of his books soared – in the first decade of publication the Romans and the Ephesians series exceeded a million copies – Dr Lloyd-Jones was still engaged in some preaching, as well as being busy in editing and doing some writing, but by 1979 he sensed deeply his time was short. He began to prepare for death.

The link between meditation and death is most pronounced in the closing days of Martyn Lloyd-Jones' life, and it is well recorded in *The Fight of Faith, 1939–1981*[11], volume 2 of Iain Murray's biography of Lloyd-Jones.

The feeble and ageing Welshman regarded preparation for death as his chief work as a Christian near the end. He acceded to Thomas Chalmers that we strangely do not give enough time to thinking about death, this one certainty! He did not count it wonderful to have a sudden death, rather he concluded that as Christians it is more important how we leave this world, since it is the time for 'a greater testimony than before'. He reminisced about the days as a boy when people were confronted more with the reality of death than they are in these modern times. With modern medicine, he said, people are living to an older age. He might have also added that people do not die at home like they used to do in yesteryear, so that we are even further removed from the Inevitable's reality.

---

11. Published by the Banner of Truth Trust, Edinburgh. Volume One is *The First Forty Years, 1899-1939*, also published by the Banner of Truth Trust.

Preparation for Death

He claimed hope for a quick death betrays our actual fear of death, whereas as believers we ought to face it manfully and be victorious over the fear of it through faith. He lamented the fact that throughout his preaching career he had not preached enough on death. Still, he was not morbid; he looked forward to the things unseen with some expectation.

Before his dying day he paid a visit to Scotland, where he spoke strongly in the Spirit though he was weak in the body, Iain Murray telling us 'the message took over the man and every last vestige of energy was poured out in both word and action'. He preached movingly for a whole hour upon the twelve verses of Psalm 2, speaking prophetically and demonstrating through his earnestness that divine wrath is a terrible reality.

Returning to London, Lloyd-Jones said death is to be faced without fear. Two things were needed in this regard: firstly, face it as a fact; secondly, Christians must be unafraid because God gives them assurance they will not be left alone. His meditation on death was not merely reserved for the words of Scripture; he clearly enjoyed meditating on the way some Christian men and women whom he had known had died. For instance, he recalled the death of William Thomas, one of the early converts at Sandfields, Wales, where Lloyd-Jones first began his long ministry of preaching and teaching. He recalled William Thomas dying of double pneumonia and how he threw his arms upwards, and with a radiant smile left the world exulting in the clear recognition of the Saviour.

As well as still being concerned for the welfare of others and possessing an unabated love for inspirational books, he had a sense of peace as the end neared, having the utmost gravity with more smiles than his authorized biographer, Iain Murray, could ever remember. He firstly did not find it easy to contemplate leaving his family as a husband, father and grandfather, but he was delivered from that anxiety through the knowledge that God is able to care for those we must leave behind.

His biographer was with him in his last days of 1981. He tells us:

He continued to give me help with the biography, though, as we spoke of things long past, he was more like an onlooker commenting on someone else's life rather than his own. He was terribly weak and losing ground. On the phone, on February 13, 1981, he thought he was 'better today', but confessed 'he had not had a very good week'. On February 19, his voice weak and husky, he spoke of being 'much the same'. It was our last conversation, for in the following week he gradually lost his strength and breath with which to speak, and communication with the family had to continue by a nod of his head, by a look or a sign and one or two very brief notes. Among his last audible words were those spoken to his consultant, Grant Williams, who visited him on February 24. Mr Williams wanted to give him some antibiotics. ML-J shook his head in disagreement. 'Well', said his doctor, 'when the Lord's time comes, even though I fill you up to the top of your head with antibiotics, it won't make any difference.' His patient still shook his head. 'I want to make you comfortable, more comfortable,' Williams went on, 'it grieves me to see you sitting here "weary and worn and sad" (quoting Bonar's well-known hymn). *'Not sad!'* The truth was he believed the work of dying was done and he was ready to go. 'Last night,' Grant Williams wrote to ML-J's local doctor on February 25, 'he refused to take any antibiotic, could hardly talk and I think he will die very shortly. I think he is very lucid and knows exactly what he wants to do.' At one point in these last days when his speech was gone, as Elizabeth (his daughter) sat beside him, he pointed her very definitely to the words of 2 Corinthians 4:16–18 which begin: *For which cause we faint not; but though our outward man perish, yet the inward man is renewed day by day. For our light affliction, which is but for a moment, worketh for us a far more exceeding and eternal weight of glory....*

'When I asked him,' says Elizabeth, 'if that was his experience now, he nodded his head with great vigour.' On Thursday evening, February 26, in a shaky hand, he wrote on a scrap of paper for Bethan (his wife) and his family: 'Do not pray for healing. Do not hold me back from the glory.' The next day he was full of smiles for the inner circle who gathered around him and by these, and gestures, he 'spoke' so clearly that one almost forgot the absence of his voice. By rolling one hand over another and pointing, he might request one of us, particularly, to speak, or, clasping his hands together to pray. On Saturday, still in his sitting-room chair, he slept some hours and at other times appeared to be unconscious. At bedtime it was clear that he was unconscious and, with only Mrs Lloyd-Jones and Ann (another daughter) present, for the first time there was a problem of not knowing how to get him to the bedroom in the front of the house. This need was met by two kindly ambulance men who responded willingly to Mrs Lloyd-Jones' call for help and put him to bed. There, a little while later, he came around and knew at once what was happening. To Bethan's inquiry whether he would like a cup of tea he nodded and, while she went to make it, Ann prayed with him. He then drank some of the tea as Bethan and Ann sat with him for about half an hour before sleeping. For over fifty years he had followed M'Cheyne's calendar for daily Bible readings, and one of those readings for the day just ended, February 28, was 1 Corinthians 15. Perhaps the conclusion of that chapter, 'Thanks be to God, which giveth us the victory through our Lord Jesus Christ,' or the words of Ann's prayer were in his consciousness as he fell quietly asleep. We cannot know for his next awakening was in 'the land of the blest'.[12]

Although the great Welsh preacher in the closing time of his life lamented somewhat at not having preached on death often enough, and confessed we do not give enough time to the subject, yet it does appear that his preparation for death, and his calm and

---

12. *The Fight of Faith, 1939–1981,* by Iain H Murray, Published by the Banner of Truth Trust, Edinburgh.

peaceful acceptance of it, did not arise from a quick 'turn-on' mentality when the occasion arose. One can see Lloyd-Jones had been actually preparing for death many years before it occurred.

Many mistakenly think they will prepare for death in years hence, just when the need arises, overlooking the truth that death needs to be looked at again and again until one becomes familiar with its terror, and in this way its terror is lessened. Says Flavel: 'We cannot be willing to go along with death, till we have some acquaintance with it; and acquainted with it we cannot be till we accustom ourselves to think assiduously and calmly about it.' (The reader will recall John Flavel's views on preparation for death have already been discussed under John Flavel.) Lloyd-Jones prepared for death a considerable time before he died, if we base this on his words spoken privately and publicly, and long years before his death there had been the peaceful resignation that God might take him at any time. Any sentiments that suddenly appear new as we read of the Welshman's closing days, any sentiments of his that suggested he had never thought that way before is understandable in the light that, until we actually know death is near, much of what we think we already know about death is expressed only in terms of seeing it from a distance.

For anyone who has sought to become familiar with death as often as possible throughout his life, can still only be familiar with it from a distance. He may be closer to understanding in knowing how to face it in a more able way than others from a long way off, but when the actual time comes to die, there is a certain chill even for the most ready.

The wonder is that God, through assurance, lessens the chill for the child of God, only we must not deceive ourselves into believing God will bring assurance when we need it, that there is no need for preparation for the Inevitable. As believers we are constantly exhorted to consider how short our life is, to think on the dimension of eternal glory. Through providence God seeks to teach us to prepare for the end. This preparation can be made easier to some extent when some acquaintance dies – the circumstances press down heavily on us and we are made to think rather forcibly. The preparation of death is somewhat made more difficult when life is smooth, when much takes us away from thinking about what is obviously certain.

It is more commendable if we prepare more willingly, yet such preparation is demanding. It requires considerable power and energy of thought to employ the mind to think on the last day. For young people it requires the most power and energy to think on it. It is trite to state no one knows when his time will come, but many of us have the senseless sentiment in practical terms:

> Men may come and men may go,
> But I go on forever.

Preparation for Eternity
What will continue to remind us all of the shortness of life and the reality of eternity? The occasional death of an acquaintance and such like? Surely, the Lord uses circumstances woven into Providence to prompt us, but there is a more frequent way possible. The occasional death of an acquaintance often loses its impact after a time.

It is no coincidence that Dr Lloyd-Jones was following M'Cheyne's calendar for daily Bible readings right up to the end of his life and was most ready for death. For over fifty years he had been following the calendar, which (you may recall) helps the reader to read the whole Bible through in one year. Such frequent reading, such extensive reading of the Word is what will prompt us to prepare for eternity, for no other writing deals with this subject as the Scriptures do; and no other writing can, as the Scriptures are the very words of God, who alone knows the true estimate of eternity and how truly short is the day of salvation.

It is not uncommon for those who read the Scriptures through at least once a year to have a greater sense of eternity than others do, others who in too many cases resort to the promise-box approach to the Word for some kind of present existential syrupy comfort. This criticism may appear unkind and even far-fetched, but it is stated with the firm conviction that it is no coincidence that in the times in which we live there has been a lamentable loss of sensitivity about eternity, as well as a signal decline in the knowledge of the Word of God.

Only the serious reader of the Word – and how serious is one who does not become familiar with all the Word often enough for all of it to influence his soul? – is well-prepared by constantly being confronted by the words of Him who decreed physical death as a punishment for sinners, but who raised His Son from death in order that we may live through the ages with Him. True, He tells us how to live in this present world, but it is, according to Him, a present *evil* world, one that seeks to deceive and take our mind off the things to come.

We must press home the uniqueness of God's Word. Other writings may gain inspiration from the Word of God itself, but they are what people of yesteryear used to call *uninspired* writings. Inspire they do, but they pale considerably against God's Word.

For an experiment take up a book written by an ordinary man – any Christian classic – and read it for a time. Then put it aside and begin reading a sizeable part of God's Word as it is contained in the Old and New Testament. Did you note the difference? Indeed, did you note the vast difference? Some have said you can tell the difference between the New Testament and those writings that followed soon after the New Testament writings were completed, such as the writings of the Apostolic Fathers. Such a difference is quite discernible between any Christian writings of any generation and the Word of God itself.

This may appear trite to those who think they already champion the cause of the uniqueness of the Scriptures, but how often many such people spend more time reading Christian books than they do the Bible! Such people may believe they cannot read the Word of God first thing each day – they believe they must ease themselves into the Word through first reading another spiritual work that takes away the jar of suddenly being confronted by the Word itself! While not decrying the value of certain Christian books – God knows many of them have been of inestimable value – one has to question his spirituality if he cannot stand 'the greater light' when it comes to reading the actual Word, and ask himself why he needs any 'lesser light' to get used to 'the greater light'. 'The greater light' may be harder to look at quite often. A believer at times may look into 'the greater light' and think it a strange, alien light, but that is only because of the lingering darkness around us and in us. We may call the lingering darkness a kind of semi-darkness for believers, but darkness it is, and it can alienate us from accepting the Scriptures as readily as we ought. Mark how readily we can take up any of those Christian books we possess, and how slow we can be in devouring great parts of the Scriptures in the way we read great parts of other writings.

It is God's Word with which primarily we ought to be familiar. 'The greater light' has the most light on the truth of eternity – in it there is no darkness. *Meditation should be occupied foremost with that which sheds the most light, the purest light.*

It is suggested Lloyd-Jones perceived this to be so, and this is why his ministry will be long remembered as one full of so much insight and truth.

CONCLUSION

The eight men who feature in this book were great, but their godliness was born out of a secretive work. As believers, pride may love us being seen as good spiritual people. Reading the Word, meditation, prayer and writing up a diary may not be practised as frequently as they ought to be for a number of reasons, but one outstanding reason is that these things are truly done best when we are not seen by men.

It is easier to pray in public than in solitariness. It is easier to be seen listening to a sermon than going off alone to ruminate on the things of God. It is easier being seen discussing spiritual issues with others than in seclusion writing a diary.

We are expected to follow the thoughts of the Father, who knows our mind and will vindicate us when it pleases Him. Even in this lifetime, if God sees we children thinking frequently on those things that are of first-rank in His mind, He will use us well since He sees us as very fit vessels here for His good purposes. The tree by the stream has potential for bringing fruit. The drawing on the water by the tree is not observable, but the secretive forces at work will produce the observable fruit.

The fruit of Baxter, Flavel, Bunyan and the others was easily observable. Even the leaves – the less major points of their character – were good.

Their lot can be ours as well. Not even Baxter, Flavel, Bunyan and the rest knew the will of God comprehensively, but whatever befell them was conducive to their salvation as well as being a blessing to many others. Anything hidden by God does not need to be known yet. God has given us a limited but perfectly sufficient knowledge concerning His will. We all have access to that 'law of the Lord'. We all are called on to delight in that law by meditating on it day and night. The blessing is for all who do so.

To be blessed means to be considered happy, fortunate, prosperous and enviable. It is the intense spiritual bliss that God gives. The psalms following Psalm One (which is like the first chapter of an intriguing novel) show us that godliness is actually worked out in the midst of many fears, frustration and failings, but whatever happens the godly man is said to prosper. Good or bad, pleasure or pain, all is grist to his mill. And not only in this life, but for the next there is hope. Whilst the wicked will be blown away like chaff as worthless and without substance, the righteous will be in the blissful congregation of all who are in right standing with God.

We know the means to such blessing. May we be blessed both here and in the hereafter for using them.